COOKSHELF

Pasta

Tom Bridge

DP
DEMPSEY
PARR

First published in Great Britain in 1998 by
Dempsey Parr
13 Whiteladies Road
Clifton
Bristol
BS8 1PB

ISBN: 1-84084-289-X

Produced by Haldane Mason, London

Acknowledgements
Art Director: Ron Samuels
Editorial Director: Sydney Francis
Managing Editor: Jo-Anne Cox
Editor: Linda A Doeser
Editorial Assistant: Elizabeth Towers
Design: dap ltd
Photography: Andrew Sydenham
Home Economist: Victoria Simister

Colour Reproduction by Inka Graphics, Cardiff

Printed in China

Note
Cup measurements in this book are for American cups.
Tablespoons are assumed to be 15 ml. Unless otherwise stated,
milk is assumed to be full fat, eggs are medium
and pepper is freshly ground black pepper.

TYPES OF PASTA

There are as many as 200 different pasta shapes and about three times as many names
for them. New shapes are being designed – and named – all the time and the same
shape may be called a different name in different regions of Italy.

anelli, anellini: *small rings for soup*

bucatini: *long, medium-thick tubes*

cannelloni: *large, thick, round pasta tubes*

capelli d'angelo: *thin strands of 'angel hair'*

conchiglie: *ridged shells*

conchigliette: *little shells*

cresti di gallo: *curved-shaped*

ditali, ditalini: *short tubes*

eliche: *loose spirals*

farfalle: *bows*

fettuccine: *medium ribbons*

fusilli: *spirals*

gemelli: *two pieces wrapped together as 'twins'*

lasagne: *flat, rectangular sheets*

linguini: *long, flat ribbons*

lumache: *snail-shaped shells*

lumaconi: *big shells*

macaroni: *long- or short-cut tubes*

orecchiette: *ear-shaped*

penne: *quill-shaped*

rigatoni: *thick, ridged tubes*

spaghetti: *fine or medium rods*

tagliarini: *thin ribbons*

tagliatelle: *broad ribbons*

vermicelli: *fine pasta, usually folded into skeins*

Cannelloni

Fusilli

Conchigliette

Conchiglie

Orecchiette tricolori

Rigatoni

Lumaconi

Fettuccine

Spaghetti

Soups & Light Meals

Pasta is so versatile: it can be used to make
soups more substantial, as a delicious and
unusual starter or as a quick and easy lunch
or light supper. The recipes in this chapter range
from traditional Italian dishes, such as
Minestrone soup and Spaghetti alla Carbonara,
to intriguing new ways with pasta, such as
Pancetta & Pecorino Cakes with Farfalle
and Pasta Omelette.

Soup recipes include filling winter dishes
that, if served with some crusty bread, make a
meal in themselves. Try Haricot Bean & Pasta
Soup, for example. Others, like Cream of
Lemon & Chicken Soup, are subtle and delicate.
Recipes for snacks and light meals offer something
for every taste – vegetable, cheese, meat and fish
sauces combined with every pasta shape from
linguine to lumache. Try Smoked Ham
Linguine if you are in a hurry, or Creamed Veal
Kidneys with Penne if you want something
a little different.

Minestrone

Serves 8–10

INGREDIENTS

3 garlic cloves
3 large onions
2 celery sticks (stalks)
2 large carrots
2 large potatoes
100 g/3^1/$_2$ oz French (green) beans
100 g/3^1/$_2$ oz courgettes (zucchini)
60 g/2 oz/4 tbsp butter

50 ml/2 fl oz/^{1}/$_4$ cup olive oil
60 g/2 oz rindless fatty bacon, finely diced
1.5 litres/2^3/$_4$ pints/6^7/$_8$ cups vegetable or chicken stock
100 g/3^1/$_2$ oz chopped tomatoes
2 tbsp tomato purée (paste)
1 bunch fresh basil, finely chopped

100 g/3^1/$_2$ oz Parmesan cheese rind
85 g/3 oz dried spaghetti, broken up
salt and pepper
freshly grated Parmesan cheese, to serve

1 Finely chop the garlic, onions, celery, carrots, potatoes, beans and courgettes (zucchini).

2 Heat the butter and oil together in a large saucepan, add the bacon and cook for 2 minutes. Add the garlic and onion and fry for 2 minutes, then stir in the celery, carrots and potatoes and fry for a further 2 minutes.

3 Add the beans to the pan and fry for 2 minutes. Stir in the courgettes (zucchini) and fry for a further 2 minutes. Cover the pan and cook all the vegetables, stirring frequently, for 15 minutes.

4 Add the stock, tomatoes, tomato purée (paste), basil, and cheese rind and season to taste. Bring to the boil, lower the heat and simmer for 1 hour. Remove and discard the cheese rind.

5 Add the spaghetti pieces to the pan and cook for 20 minutes. Serve in large, warm soup bowls sprinkled with freshly grated Parmesan cheese.

Italian Cream of Tomato Soup

Serves 4

INGREDIENTS

60 g/2 oz/4 tbsp unsalted butter	600 ml/1 pint/2¹/₂ cups vegetable stock	150 ml/¹/₄ pint/⁵/₈ cup double (heavy) cream
1 large onion, chopped	pinch of bicarbonate of soda (baking soda)	salt and pepper
900 g/2 lb Italian plum tomatoes, skinned and roughly chopped	225 g/8 oz/2 cups dried fusilli	fresh basil leaves, to garnish
	1 tbsp caster (superfine) sugar	deep-fried croûtons, to serve

1 Melt the butter in a pan and fry the onion until softened. Add the chopped tomatoes, with 300 ml/ ½ pint/1¼ cups of vegetable stock and the bicarbonate of soda (baking soda). Bring the soup to the boil and simmer for 20 minutes.

2 Remove the pan from the heat and set aside to cool. Purée the soup in a blender or food processor and pour through a fine strainer back into the saucepan.

3 Add the remaining vegetable stock and the fusilli to the pan, and season to taste.

4 Add the sugar to the pan, bring to the boil, then simmer for about 15 minutes.

5 Pour the soup into warm soup bowls, swirl the double (heavy) cream around the surface of the soup and garnish with fresh basil leaves. Serve immediately with deep-fried croûtons.

VARIATION

To make orange and tomato soup, simply use half the quantity of vegetable stock, topped up with the same amount of fresh orange juice and garnish the soup with orange rind. Or to make tomato and carrot soup, add half the quantity again of vegetable stock with the same amount of carrot juice and 175 g/6 oz/1¼ cups grated carrot to the recipe, cooking the carrot with the onion.

Potato & Parsley Soup with Pesto

Serves 4

INGREDIENTS

3 slices rindless, smoked, fatty
  bacon
450 g/1 lb floury potatoes
450 g/1 lb onions
25 g/1 oz/2 tbsp butter
600 ml/1 pint/2^1/2 cups
  chicken stock
600 ml/1 pint/2^1/2 cups milk
100 g/3^1/2 oz/^{3}/4 cup
  dried conchigliette

150 ml/^{1}/4 pint/^{5}/8 cup double
  (heavy) cream
chopped fresh parsley
freshly grated Parmesan
  cheese and garlic bread, to
  serve

PESTO SAUCE:
60 g/2 oz/1 cup finely chopped
  fresh parsley

2 garlic cloves, crushed
60 g/2 oz/^{2}/3 cup pine nuts
  (kernels), crushed
2 tbsp chopped fresh basil
  leaves
60 g/2 oz/^{2}/3 cup freshly
  grated Parmesan cheese
white pepper
150 ml/^{1}/4 pint/^{5}/8 cup
  olive oil

1 To make the pesto
sauce, process all of
the ingredients in a blender
or food processor for
2 minutes, or blend
together by hand (see
Cook's Tip).

2 Finely chop the bacon,
potatoes and onions.
Fry the bacon in a pan for
4 minutes. Stir in the
butter, potatoes and onions
and cook for 12 minutes.

3 Add the stock and milk
to the pan, bring to the
boil and simmer for
10 minutes. Add the pasta
and simmer for a further
12-14 minutes.

4 Blend in the cream and
simmer for 5 minutes.
Add the parsley and 2 tbsp
pesto sauce. Transfer the
soup to serving bowls and
serve with the Parmesan
cheese and garlic bread.

COOK'S TIP

*If you are making pesto by
hand, it is best to use a
mortar and pestle.
Thoroughly grind together
the parsley, garlic, pine nuts
(kernels) and basil to make
a smooth paste, then mix in
the cheese and pepper.
Finally, gradually beat
in the oil.*

Ravioli alla Parmigiana

Serves 4

INGREDIENTS

285 g/10 oz Basic Pasta Dough (see page 4)	FILLING:	125 ml/4 fl oz/^{1}/$_2$ cup Espagnole Sauce (see Cook's Tip, below)
1.2 litres/2 pints/5 cups veal stock	100 g/3^1/$_2$ oz/1 cup freshly grated Parmesan cheese	1 small onion, finely chopped
freshly grated Parmesan cheese, to serve	100 g/3^1/$_2$ oz/1^2/$_3$ cups fine white breadcrumbs	1 tsp freshly grated nutmeg
	2 eggs	

1 Make the basic pasta dough (see page 4). Carefully roll out 2 sheets of the pasta dough and cover with a damp tea towel (dish cloth) while you make the filling for the ravioli.

2 To make the filling, mix together the grated Parmesan cheese, white breadcrumbs, eggs, espagnole sauce (see Cook's Tip, right), chopped onion and the freshly grated nutmeg in a large mixing bowl.

3 Place spoonfuls of the filling at regular intervals on 1 sheet of pasta dough. Cover with the second sheet of pasta dough, then cut into squares and seal the edges.

4 Bring the veal stock to the boil in a large pan. Add the ravioli and cook for about 15 minutes.

5 Transfer the soup and ravioli to warm serving bowls and serve at once, generously sprinkled with Parmesan cheese.

COOK'S TIP

For espagnole sauce, melt 2 tbsp butter and stir in 25g/1 oz/^{1}/$_4$ cup plain flour until smooth. Stir in 1 tsp tomato purée, 250 ml/ 9 fl oz/1^1/$_8$ cups hot veal stock, 1 tbsp Madeira and 1^1/$_2$ tsp white wine vinegar. Dice 25 g/1 oz each bacon, carrot and onion and 15 g/ ^{1}/$_2$ oz each celery, leek and fennel. Fry with a thyme sprig and a bay leaf in oil. Drain, add to the sauce and simmer for 4 hours. Strain.

Pea & Egg Noodle Soup with Parmesan Cheese Croûtons

Serves 4

INGREDIENTS

3 slices smoked, rindless, fatty bacon, diced	2.3 litres/4 pints/10 cups chicken stock	chopped fresh parsley, to garnish
1 large onion, chopped	225 g/ 8 oz dried egg noodles	Parmesan cheese croûtons
15 g/$^1/_2$ oz/1 tbsp butter	150 ml/$^1/_4$ pint/$^5/_8$ cup double (heavy) cream	(see Cook's Tip, below), to serve
450 g/1 lb/2$^1/_2$ cups dried peas, soaked in cold water for 2 hours and drained	salt and pepper	

1 Put the bacon, onion and butter in a large pan and cook over a low heat for about 6 minutes.

2 Add the peas and the chicken stock to the pan and bring to the boil. Season lightly with salt and pepper, cover and simmer for 1½ hours.

3 Add the egg noodles to the pan and simmer for a further 15 minutes.

4 Pour in the cream and blend thoroughly. Transfer to soup bowls, garnish with parsley and top with Parmesan cheese croûtons (see Cook's Tip, right). Serve immediately.

VARIATION

Use other pulses, such as dried haricot (navy) beans, borlotti or pinto beans, instead of the peas.

COOK'S TIP

To make Parmesan cheese croûtons, cut a French stick into slices. Coat each slice lightly with olive oil and sprinkle with Parmesan cheese. Grill (broil) for about 30 seconds.

Haricot (Navy) Bean & Pasta Soup

Serves 4

INGREDIENTS

250 g/9 oz/1^1/3 cups haricot
(navy) beans, soaked for
3 hours in cold water and
drained
4 tbsp olive oil
2 large onions, sliced
3 garlic cloves, chopped
425 g/14 oz can chopped
tomatoes

1 tsp dried oregano
1 tsp tomato purée (paste)
850 ml/1^1/2 pints/3^1/2 cups
water
90 g/3^1/2 oz/^{3}/4 cup dried
fusilli or conchigliette
115 g/4 oz sun-dried
tomatoes, drained and
thinly sliced

1 tbsp chopped fresh
coriander (cilantro) or flat
leaf parsley
salt and pepper
2 tbsp Parmesan cheese
shavings, to serve

1 Put the haricot (navy) beans in a large pan. Cover with cold water and bring to the boil. Boil vigorously for 15 minutes. Drain and keep warm.

2 Heat the oil in a pan over a medium heat and fry the onions for 2–3 minutes or until soft. Stir in the garlic and cook for 1 minute. Stir in the tomatoes, oregano and tomato purée (paste).

3 Add the water and the reserved beans to the pan. Bring to the boil, cover, then simmer for about 45 minutes, or until the beans are almost tender.

4 Add the pasta to the pan and season to taste. Stir in the sun-dried tomatoes, bring back to the boil, partly cover and simmer for 10 minutes, or until the pasta is tender, but still firm to the bite.

5 Stir the herbs into the soup. Ladle the soup into warm serving bowls, sprinkle with Parmesan and serve.

COOK'S TIP

If preferred, place the beans in a pan of cold water and bring to the boil. Remove from the heat and leave the beans to cook in the water. Drain and rinse before using.

Chick Pea (Garbanzo Bean) & Chicken Soup

Serves 4

INGREDIENTS

25 g/1 oz/2 tbsp butter
3 spring onions (scallions), chopped
2 garlic cloves, crushed
1 fresh marjoram sprig, finely chopped

350 g/12 oz boned chicken breasts, diced
1.2 litres/2 pints/5 cups chicken stock
350 g/12 oz can chick peas (garbanzo beans), drained
1 bouquet garni

1 red (bell) pepper, diced
1 green (bell) pepper, diced
115 g/4 oz/1 cup small dried pasta shapes, such as elbow macaroni
salt and white pepper
croûtons, to serve

1 Melt the butter in a large saucepan. Add the spring onions (scallions), garlic, sprig of fresh marjoram and the diced chicken and cook, stirring frequently, over a medium heat for 5 minutes.

2 Add the chicken stock, chick peas (garbanzo beans) and bouquet garni to the pan and season with salt and white pepper.

3 Bring the soup to the boil, lower the heat and then simmer gently for about 2 hours.

4 Add the diced (bell) peppers and pasta to the pan, then simmer for a further 20 minutes.

5 Transfer the soup to a warm tureen. To serve, ladle the soup into individual serving bowls and serve immediately, garnished with the croûtons.

COOK'S TIP

If preferred, use dried chick peas (garbanzo beans). Cover with cold water and set aside to soak for 5–8 hours. Drain and add the peas to the soup, according to the recipe, and allow an additional 30 minutes– 1 hour cooking time.

Cream of Lemon & Chicken Soup with Spaghetti

Serves 4

INGREDIENTS

60 g/2 oz/4 tbsp butter	3 lemons	salt and white pepper
8 shallots, thinly sliced	1.2 litres/2 pints/5 cups	
2 carrots, thinly sliced	chicken stock	TO GARNISH:
2 celery sticks (stalks), thinly	225 g/8 oz dried spaghetti,	fresh parsley sprig
sliced	broken into small pieces	3 lemon slices, halved
225 g/8 oz boned chicken	150 ml/¼ pint/⅝ cup double	
breasts, finely chopped	(heavy) cream	

1 Melt the butter in a large saucepan. Add the shallots, carrots, celery and chicken and cook over a low heat, stirring occasionally, for 8 minutes.

2 Thinly pare the lemons and blanch the lemon rind in boiling water for 3 minutes. Squeeze the juice from the lemons.

3 Add the lemon rind and juice to the pan, together with the chicken stock. Bring slowly to the boil over a low heat and simmer for 40 minutes.

4 Add the spaghetti to the pan and cook for 15 minutes. Season with salt and white pepper and add the cream. Heat through, but do not allow the soup to boil.

5 Pour the soup into a tureen or individual bowls, garnish with the parsley and half slices of lemon and serve immediately.

COOK'S TIP

You can prepare this soup up to the end of step 3 in advance, so that all you need do before serving is heat it through before adding the pasta and the finishing touches.

Chicken & Sweetcorn Soup

Serves 4

INGREDIENTS

450 g/1 lb boned chicken breasts, cut into strips	150 ml/¼ pint/⅝ cup double (heavy) cream	3 tbsp milk
1.2 litres/2 pints/5 cups chicken stock	100 g/3½ oz/¾ cup dried vermicelli	175 g/6 oz sweetcorn (corn) kernels
	1 tbsp cornflour (cornstarch)	salt and pepper

1 Put the chicken, stock and cream into a large saucepan and bring to the boil over a low heat. Reduce the heat slightly and simmer for about 20 minutes. Season with salt and pepper to taste.

2 Meanwhile, cook the vermicelli in lightly salted boiling water for 10-12 minutes, until just tender. Drain the pasta and keep warm.

3 Mix together the cornflour (cornstarch) and milk to make a smooth paste, then stir into the soup until thickened.

4 Add the sweetcorn (corn) and pasta to the pan and heat through.

5 Transfer the soup to a warm tureen or individual soup bowls and serve immediately.

COOK'S TIP

If you are short of time, buy ready-cooked chicken, remove any skin and cut it into slices.

VARIATION

For crab and sweetcorn soup, substitute 450 g/1 lb cooked crabmeat for the chicken breasts. Flake the crabmeat well before adding it to the saucepan and reduce the cooking time by 10 minutes. For a Chinese-style soup, substitute egg noodles for the vermicelli and use canned, creamed sweetcorn (corn).

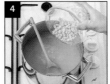

Veal & Ham Soup with Sherry

Serves 4

INGREDIENTS

60 g/2 oz/4 tbsp butter
1 onion, diced
1 carrot, diced
1 celery stick (stalk), diced
450 g/1 lb very thinly sliced
  veal
450 g/1 lb thinly sliced ham

60 g/2 oz/^{1}/$_2$ cup plain
  (all purpose) flour
1 litre/1^3/$_4$ pints/4^3/$_8$ cups
  beef stock
1 bay leaf
8 black peppercorns
pinch of salt

3 tbsp redcurrant jelly
150 ml/^{1}/$_4$ pint/^{5}/$_8$ cup cream
  sherry
100 g/3^1/$_2$ oz/^{3}/$_4$ cup dried
  vermicelli
garlic croûtons, to serve

1 Melt the butter in a large saucepan. Cook the onions, carrot, celery, veal and ham over a low heat for 6 minutes.

2 Sprinkle over the flour and cook, stirring, for a further 2 minutes. Gradually stir in the stock, then add the bay leaf, peppercorns and salt. Bring to the boil and simmer for 1 hour.

3 Remove from the heat and add the redcurrant jelly and cream sherry. Set aside for about 4 hours.

4 Discard the bay leaf from the pan and reheat the soup over a low heat until warmed through.

5 Meanwhile, cook the vermicelli in a pan of lightly salted boiling water for 10-12 minutes. Stir the vermicelli into the soup and transfer to warm soup bowls. Serve with garlic croûtons (see Cook's Tip, right).

COOK'S TIP

To make garlic croûtons, remove the crusts from 3 slices of day-old white bread. Cut the bread into 5 mm/^{1}/$_4$ inch cubes. Heat 3 tbsp olive oil over a low heat and stir-fry 1–2 finely chopped garlic cloves for 1–2 minutes. Remove the garlic and add the bread. Cook, stirring frequently, until golden brown. Remove from the pan and drain on kitchen paper (towels).

Tuscan Veal Broth

Serves 4

INGREDIENTS

60 g/2 oz/^{1}/$_3$ cup dried peas, soaked for 2 hours and drained	600 ml/1 pint/2^1/$_2$ cups water	1 red onion, finely chopped
900 g/2 lb boned neck of veal, diced	60 g/2 oz/^{1}/$_3$ cup barley, washed	100 g/3^1/$_2$ oz chopped tomatoes
1.2 litres/2 pints/5 cups beef or brown stock (see Cook's Tip)	1 large carrot, diced	1 fresh basil sprig
	1 small turnip (about 175 g/6 oz), diced	100 g/3^1/$_2$ oz/^{3}/$_4$ cup dried vermicelli
	1 large leek, thinly sliced	salt and white pepper

1 Put the peas, veal, stock and water into a large saucepan and gently bring to the boil. Using a slotted spoon, skim off any scum that rises to the surface of the liquid.

2 When all of the scum has been removed, add the barley and a pinch of salt to the mixture. Simmer gently over a low heat for 25 minutes.

3 Add the carrot, turnip, leek, onion, tomatoes and basil to the pan, and season to taste. Simmer for about 2 hours, skimming the surface from time to time. Remove the pan from the heat and set aside for 2 hours.

4 Set the pan over a medium heat and bring to the boil. Add the vermicelli and cook for 12 minutes. Season with salt and pepper to taste and remove and discard the basil. Ladle into soup bowls and serve immediately.

COOK'S TIP

Brown stock is made with veal bones and shin of beef roasted with dripping (drippings) in the oven for 40 minutes. Transfer the bones to a pan, add sliced leeks, onion, celery and carrots, a bouquet garni, white wine vinegar and a thyme sprig and cover with water. Simmer over a very low heat for 3 hours. Strain and blot the fat from the surface with kitchen paper.

Veal & Wild Mushroom Soup with Vermicelli

Serves 4

INGREDIENTS

450 g/1 lb veal, thinly sliced	pinch of mace	100 g/3¹/₂ oz/³/₄ cup dried
450 g/1 lb veal bones	140 g/5 oz oyster and shiitake	vermicelli
1.2 litres/2 pints/5 cups water	mushrooms, roughly	1 tbsp cornflour (cornstarch)
1 small onion	chopped	3 tbsp milk
6 peppercorns	150 ml/¹/₄ pint/⁵/₈ cup double	salt and pepper
1 tsp cloves	(heavy) cream	

1 Put the veal, bones and water into a large saucepan. Bring to the boil and lower the heat. Add the onion, peppercorns, cloves and mace and simmer for about 3 hours, until the veal stock is reduced by one-third.

2 Strain the stock, skim off any fat on the surface with a slotted spoon, and pour the stock into a clean saucepan. Add the veal meat to the pan.

3 Add the mushrooms and cream, bring to the boil over a low heat and simmer for 12 minutes. Meanwhile, cook the vermicelli in lightly salted boiling water until tender, but still firm to the bite. Drain and keep warm.

4 Mix together the cornflour (cornstarch) and milk to form a smooth paste. Stir into the soup to thicken. Season to taste with salt and pepper and just before serving, add the vermicelli. Transfer the soup to a warm tureen and serve immediately.

COOK'S TIP

You can make this soup with the more inexpensive cuts of veal, such as breast or neck slices. These are lean and the long cooking time ensures that the meat is really tender.

Mussel & Potato Soup

Serves 4

INGREDIENTS

750 g/1 lb 10 oz mussels	60 g/2 oz/$^{1}/_{2}$ cup plain	1 tbsp lemon juice
2 tbsp olive oil	(all purpose) flour	2 egg yolks
100 g/3$^{1}/_{2}$ oz/7 tbsp unsalted	450 g/1 lb potatoes, thinly	salt and pepper
butter	sliced	
2 slices rindless, fatty bacon,	100 g/3$^{1}/_{2}$ oz/$^{3}/_{4}$ cup	TO GARNISH:
chopped	dried conchigliette	2 tbsp finely chopped fresh
1 onion, chopped	300 ml/$^{1}/_{2}$ pint/1$^{1}/_{4}$ cups	parsley
2 garlic cloves, crushed	double (heavy) cream	lemon wedges

1 Debeard the mussels and scrub them under cold water for 5 minutes. Discard any mussels that do not close immediately when sharply tapped.

2 Bring a large pan of water to the boil, add the mussels, oil and a little pepper and cook until the mussels open.

3 Drain the mussels, reserving the cooking liquid. Discard any mussels that are closed. Remove the mussels from their shells.

4 Melt the butter in a large saucepan and cook the bacon, onion and garlic for 4 minutes. Stir in the flour, then 1.2 litres/2 pints/5 cups of the reserved cooking liquid.

5 Add the potatoes to the pan and simmer for 5 minutes. Add the conchigliette and simmer for a further 10 minutes.

6 Add the cream and lemon juice, season to taste, then add the mussels to the pan.

7 Blend the egg yolks with 1-2 tbsp of the remaining cooking liquid, stir into the pan and cook for 4 minutes.

8 Ladle the soup into 4 warm individual soup bowls, garnish with the chopped fresh parsley and lemon wedges and serve.

Italian Fish Soup

Serves 4

INGREDIENTS

60 g/2 oz/4 tbsp butter
450 g/1 lb assorted fish fillets, such as red mullet and snapper
450 g/1 lb prepared seafood, such as squid and prawns (shrimp)
225 g/8 oz fresh crabmeat
1 large onion, sliced

25 g/1 oz/^{1}/$_4$ cup plain (all purpose) flour
1.2 litres/2 pints/5 cups fish stock
100 g/3^1/$_2$ oz/^{3}/$_4$ cup dried pasta shapes, such as ditalini or elbow macaroni
1 tbsp anchovy essence

grated rind and juice of 1 orange
50 ml/2 fl oz/^{1}/$_2$ cup dry sherry
300 ml/^{1}/$_2$ pint/1^1/$_4$ cups double (heavy) cream
salt and black pepper
crusty brown bread, to serve

1 Melt the butter in a large saucepan and cook the fish fillets, seafood, crabmeat and onion over a low heat for 6 minutes.

2 Stir the flour into the mixture.

3 Gradually add the fish stock and bring to the boil, stirring constantly. Reduce the heat and simmer for 30 minutes.

4 Add the pasta and cook for 10 minutes.

5 Stir in the anchovy essence, orange rind, orange juice, sherry and double (heavy) cream. Season to taste.

6 Heat the soup until completely warmed through. Transfer the soup to a tureen or to warm soup bowls and serve with crusty brown bread.

COOK'S TIP

The heads, tails, trimmings and bones of most non-oily fish can be used to make fish stock. Simmer 900 g/2 lb fish pieces in a pan with 150 ml/5 fl oz white wine, 1 chopped onion, 1 sliced carrot, 1 sliced celery stick (stalk), 4 black peppercorns, 1 bouquet garni and 1.75 litres/3 pints/7^1/$_2$ cups water for 30 minutes, then strain.

Spaghetti alla Carbonara

Serves 4

INGREDIENTS

425 g/15 oz dried spaghetti	25 g/1 oz/2 tbsp butter	100 g /3^1/2 oz/1 cup freshly
2 tbsp olive oil	175 g/6 oz mushrooms, thinly	grated Parmesan cheese,
1 large onion, thinly sliced	sliced	plus extra to serve
2 garlic cloves, chopped	300 ml/^{1}/2 pint/1^1/4 cups	(optional)
175 g/6 oz rindless bacon, cut	double (heavy) cream	salt and pepper
into thin strips	3 eggs, beaten	fresh sage sprigs, to garnish

1 Warm a large serving dish or bowl. Bring a large pan of lightly salted water to the boil. Add the spaghetti and 1 tbsp of the oil and cook until tender, but still firm to the bite. Drain, return to the pan and keep warm.

2 Heat the remaining oil in a frying pan (skillet) over a medium heat. Add the onion and fry until it is transparent. Add the garlic and bacon and fry until the bacon is crisp. Transfer to the warm dish.

3 Melt the butter in the frying pan (skillet). Add the mushrooms and fry, stirring occasionally, for 3-4 minutes. Return the bacon mixture to the pan. Cover and keep warm.

4 Mix together the cream, eggs and cheese in a large bowl and then season to taste with salt and pepper.

5 Working very quickly, tip the spaghetti into the bacon and mushroom mixture and pour over the eggs. Toss the spaghetti quickly into the egg and cream mixture, using 2 forks. garnish and serve with extra grated Parmesan cheese, if using.

COOK'S TIP

The key to success with this recipe is not to overcook the egg. That is why it is important to keep all the ingredients hot enough just to cook the egg and to work rapidly to avoid scrambling it.

Smoked Ham Linguini

Serves 4

INGREDIENTS

450 g/1 lb dried linguini	150 ml/$^{1}/_{4}$ pint/$^{5}/_{8}$ cup Italian	salt and pepper
450 g/1 lb broccoli florets	Cheese Sauce (see Cook's	Italian bread, to serve
225g/8 oz Italian smoked ham	Tip, below right)	

1 Bring a large pan of lightly salted water to the boil. Add the linguini and broccoli florets and cook for 10 minutes, until the linguini is tender, but still firm to the bite.

2 Drain the linguini and broccoli thoroughly, set aside and keep warm.

3 Meanwhile, make the Italian Cheese Sauce (see Cook's Tip, right).

4 Using a sharp knife, cut the Italian smoked ham into thin strips. Toss the linguini, broccoli and ham into the Italian Cheese Sauce and gently warm through over a very low heat.

5 Transfer the pasta mixture to a warm serving dish. Sprinkle with black pepper and serve with Italian bread.

COOK'S TIP

There are many types of Italian bread which would be suitable to serve with this dish. Ciabatta is made with olive oil and is available plain and with different ingredients, such as olives or sun-dried tomatoes.

COOK'S TIP

For Italian Cheese Sauce, melt 2 tbsp butter in a pan. Stir in 25 g/1 oz/$^{1}/_{4}$ cup plain (all purpose) flour and cook gently until the roux is crumbly in texture. Stir in 300 ml/$^{1}/_{2}$ pint/1$^{1}/_{4}$ cups hot milk and cook for 15 minutes. Add a pinch of nutmeg, a pinch of dried thyme, 2 tbsp white wine vinegar. Season. Stir in 3 tbsp double (heavy) cream, 60 g/2 oz/$^{1}/_{2}$ cup grated Mozzarella, 60g/2 oz/ $^{2}/_{3}$ cup grated Parmesan, 1 tsp English mustard and 2 tbsp soured cream.

Chorizo & Wild Mushrooms with a Spicy Vermicelli

Serves 6

INGREDIENTS

680 g/1^{1}/$_{2}$ lb dried vermicelli	225 g/8 oz wild mushrooms	salt and pepper
125 ml/4 fl oz/^{1}/$_{2}$ cup olive oil	3 fresh red chillies, chopped	10 anchovy fillets, to garnish
2 garlic cloves	2 tbsp freshly grated	
125 g/4^{1}/$_{2}$ oz chorizo, sliced	Parmesan cheese	

1 Bring a large pan of lightly salted water to the boil. Add the vermicelli and 1 tbsp of the oil and cook until just tender, but still firm to the bite. Drain, place on a warm serving plate and keep warm.

2 Meanwhile heat the remaining oil in a large frying pan (skillet). Add the garlic and fry for 1 minute. Add the chorizo and wild mushrooms and cook for 4 minutes, then add the chopped chillies and cook for 1 further minute.

3 Pour the chorizo and wild mushroom mixture over the vermicelli and season. Sprinkle over the freshly grated Parmesan cheese, garnish with a lattice of anchovy fillets and serve immediately.

VARIATION

Fresh sardines may be used instead of the anchovies. However, ensure that you gut and clean the sardines, removing the backbone, before using them.

COOK'S TIP

Always obtain wild mushrooms from a reliable source: never pick them yourself unless you are sure of their identity. Many varieties of mushrooms are now cultivated and most are indistinguishable from the wild varieties. Mixed colour oyster mushrooms are used here, but you could also use chanterelles. However, chanterelles shrink during cooking, so you may need more.

Pancetta & Pecorino Cakes on a Bed of Farfalle

Serves 4

INGREDIENTS

25 g/1 oz/2 tbsp butter, plus extra for greasing	75 g/2³/₄ oz/⁷/₈ cup grated pecorino cheese	400 g/14 oz/3¹/₂ cups dried farfalle
100 g/3¹/₂ oz pancetta, rind removed	150 ml/¹/₄ pint/⁵/₈ cup milk, plus extra for glazing	1 tbsp olive oil
225 g/8 oz/2 cups self-raising (self-rising) flour	1 tbsp tomato ketchup	salt and black pepper
	1 tsp Worcestershire sauce	3 tbsp Pesto (see page 12) or anchovy sauce (optional)
		green salad, to serve

1 Grease a baking (cookie) sheet. Grill (broil) the pancetta until it is cooked, then allow it to cool and chop finely

2 Sift the flour and a pinch of salt into a bowl. Rub in the butter with your fingertips, then add the pancetta and one-third of the grated cheese.

3 Mix together the milk, tomato ketchup and

Worcestershire sauce and add to the dry ingredients, mixing to make a soft dough.

4 Roll out the dough on a lightly floured board to make an 18 cm/7 inch round. Brush with milk to glaze and cut into 8 wedges.

5 Arrange the dough wedges on the prepared baking (cookie) sheet and sprinkle over the

remaining cheese. Bake in a preheated oven at 200°C/400°F/Gas 6 for 20 minutes.

6 Bring a pan of lightly salted water to the boil. Add the farfalle and the oil and cook until just tender, but still firm to the bite. Drain and transfer to a serving dish. Top with the pancetta and pecorino cakes. Serve with the sauce of your choice and a salad.

Orecchiette with Bacon & Tomatoes

Serves 4

INGREDIENTS

900 g/2 lb small, sweet tomatoes	1 garlic clove, crushed	1 tbsp olive oil
6 slices rindless, smoked bacon	4 fresh oregano sprigs, finely chopped	salt and pepper
60 g/2 oz/4 tbsp butter	450 g/1 lb/4 cups dried	freshly grated Pecorino cheese, to serve
1 onion, chopped	orecchiette	fresh basil sprigs, to garnish

1 Blanch the tomatoes in boiling water. Drain, skin and seed the tomatoes, then roughly chop the flesh. Chop the bacon into small dice.

2 Melt the butter in a saucepan and fry the bacon until it is golden. Add the onion and garlic and fry for 5-7 minutes, until softened.

3 Add the tomatoes and oregano to the pan and season to taste. Lower the heat and simmer for 10-12 minutes.

4 Bring a pan of lightly salted water to the boil. Add the orecchiette and oil and cook for 12 minutes, until just tender, but still firm to the bite. Drain and transfer to a serving dish. Spoon over the bacon and tomato sauce and toss to coat. Garnish and serve.

VARIATION

You could also use 450 g/ 1 lb spicy Italian sausages. Squeeze the meat out of the skins and add to the pan in step 2 instead of the bacon.

COOK'S TIP

For an authentic Italian flavour use pancetta, rather than ordinary bacon. This kind of bacon is streaked with fat and adds rich undertones of flavour to many traditional dishes. It is available both smoked and unsmoked and can be bought in a single, large piece or cut into slices. You can buy it in some supermarkets and all Italian delicatessens.

Creamed Veal Kidneys with Penne & Pesto Sauce

Serves 4

INGREDIENTS

75 g/2³/4 oz/5 tbsp butter
12 veal kidneys, trimmed and thinly sliced
175 g/6 oz button mushrooms, sliced
1 tsp English mustard

pinch of freshly grated root ginger
2 tbsp dry sherry
150 ml/¹/4 pint/⁵/8 cup double (heavy) cream
2 tbsp Pesto Sauce (see page 12)

400 g/14 oz dried penne
1 tbsp olive oil
salt and pepper
4 slices of hot toast cut into triangles
fresh parsley sprigs, to garnish

1 Melt the butter in a frying pan (skillet) and fry the kidneys for 4 minutes. Transfer the kidneys to an ovenproof dish and keep warm.

2 Add the mushrooms to the frying pan (skillet), and cook for 2 minutes.

3 Add the mustard and ginger to the pan and season to taste. Cook for 2 minutes, then add the sherry, cream and pesto sauce. Cook for a further 3 minutes, then pour the sauce over the kidneys. Bake in a preheated oven at 190°C/375°F/ Gas 5 for 10 minutes.

4 Bring a pan of lightly salted water to the boil. Add the penne and the oil and cook until just tender, but still firm to the bite. Drain and transfer to a warm serving dish.

5 Top the pasta with the kidneys in the pesto sauce. Place triangles of warm toast around the kidneys, garnish with fresh parsley and serve.

COOK'S TIP

Store the pesto sauce in an airtight container for up to a week in the refrigerator, or freeze (before adding the Parmesan) for 3 months.

Marinated Aubergine (Eggplant) on a Bed of Linguine

Serves 4

INGREDIENTS

150 ml/¹/₄ pint/⁵/₈ cup vegetable stock	450 g/1 lb aubergine (eggplant), peeled and thinly sliced	2 tbsp chopped fresh oregano
150 ml/¹/₄ pint/⁵/₈ cup white wine vinegar	400 g/14 oz dried linguine	2 tbsp finely chopped roasted almonds
2 tsp balsamic vinegar		2 tbsp diced red (bell) pepper
3 tbsp olive oil	MARINADE:	2 tbsp lime juice
fresh oregano sprig	2 tbsp extra virgin oil	grated rind and juice of 1 orange
	2 garlic cloves, crushed	salt and pepper

1 Put the vegetable stock, wine vinegar and balsamic vinegar into a saucepan and bring to the boil over a low heat. Add 2 tsp of the olive oil and the sprig of oregano and simmer gently for about 1 minute.

2 Add the aubergine slices to the pan, remove from the heat and set aside for 10 minutes.

3 Meanwhile, make the marinade. Combine the oil, garlic, fresh oregano, almonds, (bell) pepper, lime juice, orange rind and juice and seasoning in a large bowl.

4 Remove the aubergine (eggplant) from the saucepan with a slotted spoon, and drain well. Mix the aubergine (eggplant) slices into the marinade, and set aside in the refrigerator for 12 hours.

5 Bring a pan of salted water to the boil. Add half the remaining oil and the linguine and cook until just tender. Drain the pasta and toss with the remaining oil. Arrange the pasta on a serving plate with the aubergine (eggplant) slices and the marinade and serve.

Spinach & Ricotta Shells

Serves 4

INGREDIENTS

400 g/14 oz dried lumache rigate grande	300 g/10^1/2 oz frozen spinach, thawed and drained	400 g/14 oz can chopped tomatoes, drained
5 tbsp olive oil	225 g/8 oz/1 cup ricotta cheese	1 garlic clove, crushed
60g/2 oz/1 cup fresh white breadcrumbs	pinch of freshly grated nutmeg	salt and pepper
125 ml/4 fl oz/^{1}/2 cup milk		

1 Bring a large saucepan of lightly salted water to the boil. Add the lumache and 1 tbsp of the olive oil and cook until just tender, but still firm to the bite. Drain the pasta, refresh under cold water and set aside.

2 Put the breadcrumbs, milk and 3 tbsp of the remaining olive oil in a food processor and work to combine.

3 Add the spinach and ricotta cheese to the food processor and work to a smooth mixture. Transfer to a bowl, stir in the nutmeg, and season with salt and pepper to taste.

4 Mix together the tomatoes, garlic and remaining oil and spoon the mixture into the base of an ovenproof dish.

5 Using a teaspoon, fill the lumache with the spinach and ricotta mixture and arrange on top of the tomato mixture in the dish. Cover and bake in a preheated oven at 180°C/350°F/Gas 4 for 20 minutes. Serve hot.

COOK'S TIP

Ricotta is a creamy Italian cheese traditionally made from ewes' milk whey. It is soft and white, with a smooth texture and a slightly sweet flavour. It should be used within 2–3 days of purchase.

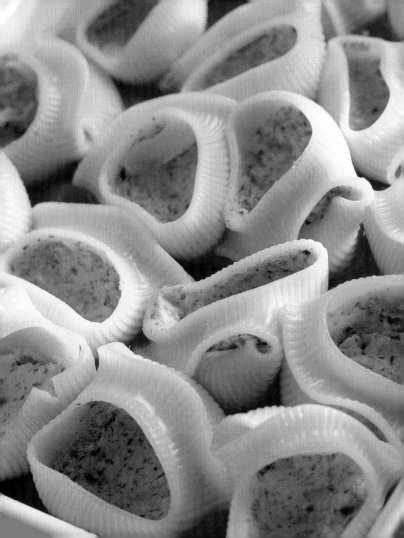

Rotelle with Spicy Italian Sauce

Serves 4

INGREDIENTS

200 ml/7 fl oz/^{7}/8 cup Italian Red Wine Sauce (see Cook's Tip)	5 tbsp olive oil 3 garlic cloves, crushed 2 fresh red chillies, chopped 1 green chilli, chopped	400 g/14 oz/3^1/2 cups dried rotelle salt and pepper warm Italian bread, to serve

1 Make the Italian Red Wine Sauce (see Cook's Tip, right).

2 Heat 4 tbsp of the oil in a pan and fry the garlic and chillies for 3 minutes.

3 Stir in the Italian Red Wine Sauce, season to taste and simmer gently for 20 minutes.

4 Bring a large saucepan of lightly salted water to the boil. Add the rotelle and the remaining oil and cook for 8 minutes, until just tender. Drain the pasta.

5 Toss the rotelle in the spicy sauce, transfer to a warm serving dish and serve immediately.

COOK'S TIP

Take care when using fresh chillies as they can burn your skin. Handle them as little as possible – wear rubber gloves if necessary. Always wash your hands afterwards and don't touch your face or eyes before you have washed your hands. Remove chilli seeds before chopping the chillies, as they are the hottest part.

COOK'S TIP

For Italian Red Wine Sauce, first make a demi-glace sauce: mix 150 ml/^{1}/4 pint/^{5}/8 cup each Brown Stock (see page 28) and Espagnole Sauce (see page 14), cook for 10 minutes and strain. Mix 125 ml/ 4 fl oz/^{1}/2 cup red wine, 2 tbsp red wine vinegar, 4 tbsp chopped shallots, 1 bay leaf and 1 thyme sprig in a pan. Bring to the boil and reduce by three-quarters. Add the demi-glace sauce and simmer for 20 minutes. Season and strain.

Tricolour Timballini

Serves 4

INGREDIENTS

15 g/¹/₂ oz/1 tbsp butter, softened	1 egg yolk	150 ml/¹/₄ pint/⁵/₈ cup dry white wine
60 g/2 oz/1 cup dried white breadcrumbs	125 g/4 oz/1 cup grated Gruyère (Swiss) cheese	150 ml/¹/₄ pint/⁵/₈ cup passata (sieved tomatoes)
175 g/6 oz dried tricolour spaghetti, broken into 5 cm/2 inch lengths	300 ml/¹/₂ pint/1¹/₄ cups Béchamel Sauce (see page 166)	1 tbsp tomato purée (paste)
3 tbsp olive oil	1 onion, finely chopped	salt and pepper
	1 bay leaf	fresh basil leaves, to garnish

1 Grease four 180 ml/6 fl oz/³/₄ cup ramekins with the butter. Evenly coat the insides with half the breadcrumbs.

2 Bring a pan of lightly salted water to the boil. Add the spaghetti and 1 tbsp of the oil and cook until just tender. Drain and transfer to a mixing bowl.

3 Add the egg yolk and cheese to the pasta and season. Pour the Béchamel sauce into the bowl and mix. Spoon the mixture into the ramekins and sprinkle over the remaining breadcrumbs.

4 Stand the ramekins on a baking (cookie) sheet and bake in a preheated oven at 220°C/425°F/Gas 7 for 20 minutes. Set aside for 10 minutes.

5 To make the sauce, heat the remaining oil in a pan and gently fry the onion and bay leaf for 2-3 minutes.

6 Stir in the wine, passata (sieved tomatoes) and tomato purée (paste). Season and simmer for 20 minutes, until thickened. Discard the bay leaf.

7 Turn the timballini out on to individual serving plates, garnish with the basil leaves and serve with the tomato sauce.

Tagliarini with Gorgonzola

Serves 4

INGREDIENTS

25 g/1 oz/2 tbsp butter
225 g/8 oz Gorgonzola cheese, roughly crumbled
150 ml/1/4 pint/5/8 cup double (heavy) cream

30 ml/2 tbsp dry white wine
1 tsp cornflour (cornstarch)
4 fresh sage sprigs, finely chopped
400 g/14 oz dried tagliarini

2 tbsp olive oil
salt and white pepper
fresh herb sprigs, to garnish

1 Melt the butter in a heavy-based saucepan. Stir in 175 g/6 oz of the Gorgonzola and melt, over a low heat, for 2 minutes.

2 Add the cream, wine and cornflour (cornstarch) and beat with a whisk until fully incorporated.

3 Stir in the sage and season to taste. Bring to the boil over a low heat, whisking constantly, until the sauce thickens. Remove from the heat and set aside.

4 Bring a large saucepan of lightly salted water to the boil. Add the tagliarini and 1 tbsp of the olive oil. Cook the pasta for 12–14 minutes or until just tender, drain thoroughly and toss in the remaining olive oil. Transfer the pasta to a serving dish and keep warm.

5 Reheat the sauce over a low heat, whisking constantly. Spoon the Gorgonzola sauce over the tagliarini, sprinkle over the remaining cheese, garnish and serve.

COOK'S TIP

Gorgonzola is one of the world's oldest veined cheeses and, arguably, its finest. When buying, always check that it is creamy yellow with delicate green veining. Avoid hard or discoloured cheese. It should have a rich, piquant aroma, not a bitter smell. If you find Gorgonzola too strong or rich, you could substitute Danish blue.

Gnocchi Piemontese

Serves 4

INGREDIENTS

450 g/1 lb warm mashed
  potato
75 g/2³/4 oz/⁵/8 cup self-
  raising (self-rising) flour
1 egg

2 egg yolks
1 tbsp olive oil
150 ml/¹/4 pint/⁵/8 cup
  Espagnole Sauce
  (see page 14)

60 g/2 oz/4 tbsp butter
175 g/6 oz/2 cups freshly
  grated Parmesan cheese
salt and pepper
fresh herbs, to garnish

1 Combine the mashed
  potato and flour in a
bowl. Add the egg and egg
yolks, season well and mix
together to form a dough.

2 Break off pieces and
  roll between the palms
of your hands to form
small balls the size of a
walnut. Flatten the balls
with a fork into the shape
of small cylinders.

3 Bring a pan of lightly
  salted water to the
boil. Add the gnocchi and
olive oil and poach for
10 minutes.

4 Mix the Espagnole
  sauce (see page 14) and
the butter in a large
saucepan over a gentle heat.
Gradually blend in the
grated Parmesan cheese.

5 Remove the gnocchi
  from the pan and toss
in the sauce, transfer to
individual serving plates,
garnish and serve.

COOK'S TIP

*This dish also makes an
excellent main meal with a
crisp salad.*

VARIATION

*These gnocchi would also
taste delicious with a tomato
sauce, in Trentino-style.
Mix together 115 g/4 oz/
1 cup finely chopped sun-
dried tomatoes, 1 finely
sliced celery stick (stalk),
1 crushed garlic clove and
6 tbsp red wine in a pan.
Cook over a low heat for
15–20 minutes. Stir in
8 skinned, chopped, Italian
plum tomatoes, season to
taste with salt and pepper
and simmer over a low heat
for a further 10 minutes.*

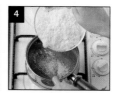

Pasta Omelette

Serves 2

INGREDIENTS

4 tbsp olive oil	1 tbsp chopped fresh flat leaf	2 tbsp stuffed green olives,
1 small onion, chopped	parsley	halved
1 fennel bulb, thinly sliced	pinch of chilli powder	salt and pepper
125 g/4^1/2 oz potato, diced	100 g/3^1/2 oz cooked short	fresh marjoram sprigs, to
1 garlic clove, chopped	pasta	garnish
4 eggs		tomato salad, to serve

1 Heat half the oil in a frying pan (skillet) and fry the onion, fennel and potato, stirring, for 8-10 minutes, until the potato is just tender.

2 Add the garlic and fry for 1 minute. Remove the pan from the heat and transfer the vegetables to a plate and set aside.

3 Beat the eggs until they are frothy. Stir in the parsley and season with salt, pepper and a pinch of chilli powder.

4 Heat 1 tbsp of the remaining oil in a clean frying pan (skillet). Add half of the egg mixture to the pan, then add the cooked vegetables, pasta and half of the olives. Pour in the remaining egg mixture and cook until the sides begin to set.

5 Lift up the edges of the omelette with a palette knife (spatula) to allow the uncooked egg to spread underneath. Cook until the underside is a light golden brown colour.

6 Slide the omelette out of the pan on to a plate. Wipe the pan with kitchen paper (kitchen towels) and heat the remaining oil. Invert the omelette into the pan and cook until the other side is golden brown.

7 Slide the omelette on to a warmed serving dish and garnish with the remaining olives and the fresh marjoram sprigs. Cut the omelette into wedges and serve with a tomato salad.

Spaghetti with Ricotta Cheese

Serves 4

INGREDIENTS

350 g/12 oz dried spaghetti	125 g/4¹/₂ oz/¹/₂ cup ricotta	125 ml/4 fl oz hot chicken
3 tbsp olive oil	cheese	stock
40 g/¹/₂ oz/3 tbsp butter	pinch of grated nutmeg	1 tbsp pine nuts (kernels)
2 tbsp chopped fresh flat leaf	pinch of ground cinnamon	salt and pepper
parsley	150 ml/¹/₄ pint/⁵/₈ cup crème	fresh flat leaf parsley sprigs,
125 g/4¹/₂ oz/1 cup freshly	fraîche (unsweetened	to garnish
ground almonds	yogurt)	

1 Bring a large pan of lightly salted water to the boil. Add the spaghetti and 1 tbsp of the oil and cook until tender, but still firm to the bite.

2 Drain the pasta, return to the pan and toss with the butter and chopped parsley. Set aside and keep warm.

3 To make the sauce, mix together the ground almonds, ricotta cheese, nutmeg, cinnamon and crème fraîche (unsweetened yogurt) over a low heat to form a thick paste. Stir in the remaining oil, then gradually stir in the hot chicken stock, until smooth. Season to taste.

4 Transfer the spaghetti to a warm serving dish, pour over the sauce and toss together well (see Cook's Tip, right). Sprinkle over the pine nuts (kernels), garnish with the flat leaf parsley sprigs and serve warm.

COOK'S TIP

Use two large forks to toss spaghetti or other long pasta, so that it is thoroughly coated with the sauce. Special spaghetti forks are available from some cookware departments and kitchen shops. Holding one fork in each hand, gently ease the prongs under the pasta on each side and lift them towards the centre. Continue until the pasta is completely coated.

Gnocchi Romana

Serves 4

INGREDIENTS

700 ml/1¹/4 pints/3¹/8 cups milk	90 g/3 oz/6 tbsp butter, plus extra for greasing	2 eggs, beaten
pinch of freshly grated nutmeg	250 g/8 oz/1¹/4 cups semolina	60 g/2 oz/¹/2 cup grated Gruyère (Swiss) cheese
	125 g/4¹/2 oz/1¹/2 cups grated Parmesan cheese	salt and pepper
		fresh basil sprigs, to garnish
---

1 Bring the milk to the boil in a saucepan. Remove from the heat and stir in the nutmeg, 25 g/1 oz/2 tbsp of the butter and salt and pepper to taste.

2 Stir the semolina into the milk, whisking to prevent lumps forming, and return the pan to a low heat. Simmer, stirring constantly, for about 10 minutes, until very thick.

3 Beat 60 g/2 oz/²/3 cup of Parmesan into the semolina mixture, then beat in the eggs. Continue beating until smooth. Set the mixture aside for a few minutes to cool slightly.

4 Spread out the semolina mixture in a smooth, even layer, about 1 cm/½ inch thick, on a sheet of baking parchment or in a large oiled baking tin (pan). Leave to cool completely, then chill in the refrigerator for 1 hour.

5 Once chilled, cut out rounds of gnocchi, measuring 4 cm/1½ inches in diameter, using a plain, greased pastry cutter.

6 Grease a shallow ovenproof dish and lay the gnocchi trimmings in the base of the dish. Cover with overlapping rounds of gnocchi.

7 Melt the remaining butter and drizzle over the gnocchi. Sprinkle over the remaining Parmesan, then sprinkle over the Gruyère (Swiss) cheese. Bake in a preheated oven at 200°C/400°F/Gas 6 for 25-30 minutes, until the top is crisp and golden brown. Garnish with the basil and serve.

Three Cheese Bake

Serves 4

INGREDIENTS

butter, for greasing	4 fresh basil sprigs	salt and black pepper
400 g/14 oz dried penne	100 g/3¹/₂ oz/1 cup grated	fresh basil leaves (optional), to
1 tbsp olive oil	mozzarella or halloumi	garnish
2 eggs, beaten	cheese	
350 g/12 oz/1¹/₂ cups ricotta	4 tbsp freshly grated	
cheese	Parmesan cheese	

1 Lightly grease an ovenproof dish.

2 Bring a large pan of lightly salted water to the boil. Add the penne and olive oil and cook until just tender, but still firm to the bite. Drain the pasta, set aside and keep warm.

3 Beat the eggs into the ricotta cheese and season to taste with salt and pepper.

4 Spoon half of the penne into the base of the dish and cover with half of the basil leaves.

5 Spoon over half of the ricotta cheese mixture. Sprinkle over the mozzarella or halloumi cheese and top with the remaining basil leaves. Cover with the remaining penne and then spoon over the remaining ricotta cheese mixture. Lightly sprinkle over the grated Parmesan cheese.

6 Bake in a preheated oven at 190°C/375°F/ Gas 5 for about 30–40 minutes, until golden brown and the cheese topping is hot and bubbling. Garnish with fresh basil leaves, if liked, and serve hot.

VARIATION

Try substituting smoked Bavarian cheese for the mozzarella or halloumi and grated Cheddar cheese for the Parmesan, for a slightly different but just as delicious flavour.

Baked Rigatoni Filled with Tuna & Ricotta Cheese

Serves 4

INGREDIENTS

butter, for greasing	225 g/ 8 oz ricotta cheese	125 g/4 oz sun-dried
450 g/1 lb dried rigatoni	125 ml/4 fl oz/¹/₂ cup double	tomatoes, drained and
1 tbsp olive oil	(heavy) cream	sliced
200 g /7 oz can flaked tuna,	225 g/8 oz/2²/₃ cups grated	salt and pepper
drained	Parmesan cheese	

1 Lightly grease an ovenproof dish.

2 Bring a large saucepan of lightly salted water to the boil. Add the rigatoni and olive oil and cook until just tender, but still firm to the bite. Drain the pasta and set aside until cool enough to handle.

3 In a bowl, mix together the tuna and ricotta cheese to form a soft paste. Spoon the mixture into a piping bag and use to fill the rigatoni. Arrange the filled pasta tubes side by side in the prepared ovenproof dish.

4 To make the sauce, mix the cream and Parmesan cheese and season. Spoon the sauce over the rigatoni and top with the sun-dried tomatoes arranged in a criss-cross pattern. Bake in a preheated oven at 200°C/400°F/Gas 6 for 20 minutes. Serve hot straight from the dish.

VARIATION

For a vegetarian version of this recipe, simply substitute a mixture of stoned (pitted) and chopped black olives and chopped walnuts for the tuna. Follow exactly the same cooking method.

Spaghetti with Anchovy & Pesto Sauce

Serves 4

INGREDIENTS

90 ml/3 fl oz olive oil	2 tbsp finely chopped fresh	salt and pepper
2 garlic cloves, crushed	oregano	2 fresh oregano sprigs, to
60 g/2 oz can anchovy fillets,	90 g/3 oz/1 cup grated	garnish
drained	Parmesan cheese, plus	
450 g/1 lb dried spaghetti	extra for serving (optional)	
60 g/2 oz Pesto Sauce (see		
page 12)		

1 Heat 1 tbsp of the oil in a small saucepan. Add the garlic and fry for 3 minutes.

2 Add the anchovies and cook, stirring, until the anchovies have disintegrated.

3 Bring a large saucepan of lightly salted water to the boil. Add the spaghetti and the remaining olive oil and cook until just tender, but still firm to the bite.

4 Add the Pesto Sauce (see page 12) and chopped fresh oregano to the anchovy mixture and then season with black pepper to taste.

5 Drain the spaghetti, using a slotted spoon, and transfer to a warm serving dish. Pour the Pesto Sauce over the spaghetti and then sprinkle over the grated Parmesan cheese. Garnish with oregano sprigs and serve with extra cheese, if using.

VARIATION

For a vegetarian version of this recipe, substitute drained sun-dried tomatoes for the anchovy fillets.

COOK'S TIP

If you find canned anchovies much too salty, soak them in a saucer of cold milk for 5 minutes, drain and pat dry with kitchen paper (kitchen towels) before using.

Fettuccine with Anchovy & Spinach Sauce

Serves 4

INGREDIENTS

900 g/2 lb fresh, young spinach leaves	6 tbsp olive oil	8 canned anchovy fillets, drained and chopped
400 g/14 oz dried fettuccine	3 tbsp pine nuts (kernels)	salt
	3 garlic cloves, crushed	

1 Trim off any tough spinach stalks. Rinse the spinach leaves and place them in a large saucepan with only the water that is clinging to them after washing. Cover and cook over a high heat, shaking the pan from time, until the spinach has wilted, but retains its colour. Drain well, set aside and keep warm.

2 Bring a large saucepan of lightly salted water to the boil. Add the fettuccine and 1 tbsp of the oil and cook for 2–3 minutes until it is just tender, but still firm to the bite.

3 Heat 4 tbsp of the remaining oil in a saucepan. Add the pine nuts (kernels) and fry until golden. Remove from the pan and set aside.

4 Add the garlic to the pan and fry until golden. Add the anchovies and stir in the spinach. Cook, stirring, for 2–3 minutes, until heated through. Return the pine nuts (kernels) to the pan.

5 Drain the fettuccine, toss in the remaining olive oil and transfer to a warm serving dish. Spoon the anchovy and spinach sauce over the fettucine, toss lightly and serve immediately.

COOK'S TIP

If you are in a hurry, use frozen spinach. Thaw and drain it thoroughly, pressing out as much moisture as possible. Cut the leaves into strips and add to the dish with the anchovies in step 4.

Penne with Muscoli Fritti nell' Olio

Serves 4–6

INGREDIENTS

400/14 oz 3^1/2 cups dried penne	1 tsp sea salt	TO GARNISH:
125 ml/4 fl oz/^{1}/2 cup olive oil	90 g/3 oz/^{2}/3 cup flour	1 lemon, thinly sliced
450 g/1 lb mussels, cooked and shelled	100 g/3^1/2 oz sun-dried tomatoes, sliced	fresh basil leaves
	salt and pepper	

1 Bring a large pan of lightly salted water to the boil. Add the penne and 1 tbsp of the olive oil and cook until the pasta is just tender, but still firm to the bite.

2 Drain the pasta and place in a warm serving dish. Set aside and keep warm.

3 Sprinkle the mussels with the sea salt. Season the flour with salt and pepper, sprinkle into a bowl and toss the mussels in the flour until coated.

4 Heat the remaining oil in a frying pan (skillet) and fry the mussels until golden brown, stirring.

5 Toss the mussels with the penne and sprinkle with the sun-dried tomatoes. Garnish with lemon slices and basil leaves and serve.

VARIATION

You could substitute clams for the mussels. If using fresh clams, try smaller varieties, such as Venus.

COOK'S TIP

Sun-dried tomatoes have been used in Mediterranean countries for a long time, but have become popular elsewhere only quite recently. They are dried and then preserved in oil. They have a concentrated, almost roasted flavour and a dense texture. They should be drained and chopped or sliced before using.

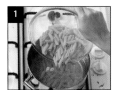

Meat & Poultry

Pasta and meat or poultry is a classic
combination. Dishes range from easy,
economic mid-week suppers to sophisticated
and elegant meals for special occasions.
The recipes in this chapter include many family
favourites, such as Spaghetti Bolognese, Fresh
Spaghetti with Italian Meatballs in Tomato
Sauce, Lasagne Verde and Stuffed Cannelloni.
There are also some exciting variations on
traditional themes, such as Sicilian Spaghetti,
Beef & Pasta Bake and Stir-fried Pork
with Pasta & Vegetables. Finally, there is a
superb collection of mouth-watering original
recipes. Why not try Fettuccine with Fillet
of Veal & Pink Grapefruit in a Rose Petal
Butter Sauce, Orecchioni with Pork in Cream
Sauce, garnished with Quail Eggs,
Chicken & Lobster on a Bed of Penne,
or Rigatoni & Pesto Baked Partridge?
You will be astonished at how quickly
and easily you can prepare these
gourmet dishes.

Spaghetti Bolognese

Serves 4

INGREDIENTS

3 tbsp olive oil
2 garlic cloves, crushed
1 large onion, finely chopped
1 carrot, diced
225 g/8 oz/2 cups lean minced
    (ground) beef, veal or
    chicken

85 g/3 oz chicken livers,
    finely chopped
100 g/3¹/₂ oz lean, Parma ham
    (prosciutto), diced
150 ml/¹/₄ pint/⁵/₈ cup
    Marsala

285 g/10 oz can chopped
    plum tomatoes
1 tbsp chopped fresh basil
    leaves
2 tbsp tomato purée (paste)
salt and pepper
450 g/1 lb dried spaghetti

1 Heat 2 tbsp of the olive oil in a large saucepan. Add the garlic, onion and carrot and fry for 6 minutes.

2 Add the minced (ground) beef, veal or chicken, chicken livers and Parma ham (prosciutto) to the pan and cook over a medium heat for 12 minutes, until well browned.

3 Stir in the Marsala, tomatoes, basil and tomato purée (paste) and cook for 4 minutes. Season to taste with salt and pepper. Cover and simmer for about 30 minutes.

4 Remove the lid from the pan, stir and simmer for a further 15 minutes.

5 Meanwhile, bring a large pan of lightly salted water to the boil. Add the spaghetti and the remaining oil and cook for about 12 minutes, until tender, but still firm to the bite. Drain and transfer to a serving dish. Pour the sauce over the pasta, toss and serve hot.

VARIATION

Chicken livers are an essential ingredient in a classic Bolognese sauce to which they add richness. However, if you prefer not to use them, you can substitute the same quantity of minced (ground) beef.

Creamed Strips of Sirloin with Rigatoni

Serves 4

INGREDIENTS

75 g/3 oz/6 tbsp butter
450 g/1 lb sirloin steak,
    trimmed and cut into thin
    strips
175 g/6 oz button
    mushrooms, sliced
1 tsp mustard

pinch of freshly grated root
    ginger
2 tbsp dry sherry
150 ml/^{1}/$_4$ pint/^{5}/$_8$ cup double
    (heavy) cream
salt and pepper
4 slices hot toast, cut into
    triangles, to serve

PASTA:
450 g/1 lb dried rigatoni
2 tbsp olive oil
2 fresh basil sprigs
115 g/4 oz/8 tbsp butter

1 Melt the butter in a frying pan (skillet) and fry the steak over a low heat for 6 minutes. Transfer to an ovenproof dish and keep warm.

2 Add the mushrooms to the remaining juices in the frying pan (skillet) and cook for 2–3 minutes. Add the mustard, ginger, salt and pepper. Cook for 2 minutes, then add the sherry and cream. Cook for 3 minutes, then pour the cream sauce over the steak.

3 Bake the steak and cream mixture in a preheated oven at 90°C/375°F/Gas 5 for 10 minutes.

4 Bring a pan of lightly salted water to the boil. Add the rigatoni, olive oil and 1 basil sprig and boil for 10 minutes. Drain and transfer to a warm serving plate. Toss the pasta with the butter, garnish with the remaining basil sprig.

5 Serve the steak with the pasta and triangles of warm toast. Serve the rigatoni separately.

Fresh Spaghetti with Italian Meatballs in Tomato Sauce

Serves 4

INGREDIENTS

150 g/5^1/2 oz/2^1/2 cups brown
    breadcrumbs
150 ml/^{1}/4 pint/^{5}/8 cup milk
25 g/1 oz/2 tbsp butter
25 g/1 oz/^{1}/4 cup wholemeal
    (whole-wheat) flour
200 ml/7 fl oz/^{7}/8 cup beef
    stock

400 g/14 oz can chopped
    tomatoes
2 tbsp tomato purée (paste)
1 tsp sugar
1 tbsp finely chopped fresh
    tarragon
1 large onion, chopped

450 g/1 lb/4 cups minced
    steak
1 tsp paprika
4 tbsp olive oil
450 g/1 lb fresh spaghetti
salt and pepper
fresh tarragon sprigs, to
    garnish

1 Soak the breadcrumbs and the milk in a bowl for 30 minutes.

2 Melt half the butter in a pan. Stir in the flour for 2 minutes. Gradually stir in the beef stock and cook, stirring, for a further 5 minutes. Add the tomatoes, tomato purée (paste), sugar and tarragon. Season well and simmer for 25 minutes.

3 Mix the onion, steak and paprika into the breadcrumbs and season. Shape into 14 meatballs.

4 Fry the meatballs in the oil and remaining butter until brown all over. Place them in a casserole, pour over the tomato sauce, cover and bake in a preheated oven at 180°C/ 350°F/Gas 4 for 25 minutes.

5 Bring a pan of lightly salted water to the boil and cook the spaghetti for 2–3 minutes, until tender, but still firm to the bite.

6 Remove the meatballs from the oven and allow them to cool for 3 minutes. Serve the meatballs and their sauce with the spaghetti, garnished with fresh tarragon sprigs.

Layered Meat Loaf

Serves 6

INGREDIENTS

25 g/1 oz/2 tbsp butter, plus extra for greasing	25 g/1 oz/1¹/₂ cup white breadcrumbs	250 ml/8 fl oz/1 cup Italian Cheese Sauce (see page 38)
1 small onion, finely chopped	¹/₂ tsp cayenne pepper	4 bay leaves
1 small red (bell) pepper, cored, seeded and chopped	1 tbsp lemon juice	175 g/6 oz fatty bacon, rinds removed
1 garlic clove, chopped	¹/₂ tsp grated lemon rind	salt and pepper
450 g/1 lb/4 cups minced (ground) beef	2 tbsp chopped fresh parsley	salad leaves (greens), to garnish
	90 g/3 oz/³/₄ cup dried short pasta, such as fusilli	
	1 tbsp olive oil	

1 Preheat the overn to 180°C/ 350°F/Gas 4. Melt the butter in a pan and fry the onion and (bell) pepper for 3 minutes. Stir in the garlic and cook for 1 minute.

2 Mash the meat with a wooden spoon until sticky. Mix in the onion mixture, breadcrumbs, cayenne pepper, lemon juice, lemon rind, parsley and seasoning.

3 Bring a pan of salted water to the boil. Add the pasta and oil and cook for 8–10 minutes. Drain and stir into the Italian Cheese Sauce.

4 Grease a 1 kg/2 lb loaf tin (pan) and arrange the bay leaves in the base. Stretch the bacon slices and use to line the base and sides of the tin (pan). Spoon in half the meat mixture and smooth the

surface. Cover with the pasta mixed with Italian Cheese Sauce, then spoon in the remaining meat mixture. Level the top and cover with foil.

5 Bake the meat loaf for 1 hour or until the juices run clear when a skewer is inserted in the centre. Pour off any excess fat and turn out the loaf on to a serving dish. Garnish with salad leaves (greens).

Egg Noodles with Beef

Serves 4

INGREDIENTS

285 g/10 oz egg noodles
3 tbsp walnut oil
2.5 cm/1 inch piece fresh root
ginger, cut into thin strips
5 spring onions (scallions),
finely shredded
2 garlic cloves, finely chopped

1 red (bell) pepper, cored,
seeded and thinly sliced
100 g/3½ oz button
mushrooms, thinly sliced
340 g/12 oz fillet steak, cut
into thin strips
1 tbsp cornflour (cornstarch)
5 tbsp dry sherry

3 tbsp soy sauce
1 tsp soft brown sugar
225 g/8 oz/1 cup beansprouts
1 tbsp sesame oil
salt and pepper
spring onion (scallion) strips,
to garnish

1 Bring a large saucepan of water to the boil. Add the noodles and cook according to the instructions on the packet. Drain and set aside.

2 Heat the walnut oil in a preheated wok. Add the ginger, spring onions (scallions) and garlic and stir-fry for 45 seconds. Add the (bell) pepper, mushrooms and steak and stir-fry for 4 minutes. Season to taste.

3 Mix together the cornflour (cornstarch), sherry and soy sauce in a small jug to form a paste, and pour into the wok. Sprinkle over the brown sugar and stir-fry all of the ingredients for 2 minutes.

4 Add the beansprouts, drained noodles and sesame oil to the wok, stir and toss together for 1 minute. Garnish with strips of spring onion (scallion) and serve.

COOK'S TIP

If you do not have a wok, you could prepare this dish in a frying pan (skillet). However, a wok is preferable, as the round base ensures an even distribution of heat and it is easier to keep stirring and tossing the contents when stir-frying.

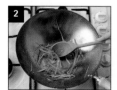

Tagliarini with Meatballs in Red Wine & Oyster Mushroom Sauce

Serves 4

INGREDIENTS

150 g/5 oz/2 cups white breadcrumbs
150 ml/^{1}/4 pint/^{5}/8 cup milk
225 g/8 oz/3 cups sliced oyster mushrooms
25 g/1 oz/2 tbsp butter
9 tbsp olive oil
25 g/1 oz/^{1}/4 cup wholemeal (whole-wheat) flour

200 ml/7 fl oz/^{7}/8 cup beef stock
150 ml/^{1}/4 pint/^{5}/8 cup red wine
4 tomatoes, skinned and chopped
1 tbsp tomato purée (paste)
1 tsp brown sugar

1 tbsp finely chopped fresh basil
12 shallots, chopped
450 g/1 lb/4 cups minced (ground) steak
1 tsp paprika
450 g/1 lb dried egg tagliarini
salt and pepper
fresh basil sprigs, to garnish

1 Soak the breadcrumbs in the milk for 30 minutes.

2 Fry the mushrooms in half the butter and 4 tbsp of the oil until soft. Stir in the flour. Add the stock and wine and simmer for 15 minutes. Add the tomatoes, tomato purée (paste), sugar and basil and simmer for 30 minutes.

3 Mix the shallots, steak and paprika with the breadcrumbs. Season then shape into 14 meatballs.

4 Heat 4 tbsp of the remaining oil and the butter in a frying pan (skillet). Fry the meatballs until brown all over. Transfer to a casserole, pour over the red wine and the mushroom sauce, cover and bake in a preheated oven at 180°C/350°F/Gas 4 for 30 minutes.

5 Bring a pan of salted water to the boil. Add the pasta and the remaining oil and cook until tender. Drain and transfer to a serving dish. Pour the meatballs and sauce on to the pasta. Garnish with fresh basil sprigs and serve.

Sicilian Spaghetti

Serves 4

INGREDIENTS

150 ml/¼ pint/⅝ cup olive oil, plus extra for brushing
2 aubergines (eggplants)
350 g/12 oz/3 cups minced (ground) beef
1 onion, chopped
2 garlic cloves, crushed
2 tbsp tomato purée (paste)

400 g/14 oz can chopped tomatoes
1 tsp Worcestershire sauce
1 tsp chopped fresh marjoram or oregano or ½ tsp dried marjoram or oregano
60 g/2 oz/½ cup stoned (pitted) black olives, sliced

1 green, red or yellow (bell) pepper, cored, seeded and chopped
175 g/6 oz dried spaghetti
115 g/4 oz/1 cup freshly grated Parmesan cheese
salt and pepper

1 Brush a 20 cm/8 inch loose-based round cake tin (pan) with oil, line the base with baking parchment and brush with oil.

2 Slice the aubergines (eggplants). Fry the aubergines (eggplant) in a little oil until browned on both sides. Drain on kitchen paper (towels).

3 Cook the beef, onion and garlic in a pan, stirring, until browned. Add the tomato purée (paste), tomatoes, Worcestershire sauce, herbs and salt and pepper. Simmer for 10 minutes. Add the olives and (bell) pepper and cook for a further 10 minutes.

4 Bring a pan of salted water to the boil. Add the spaghetti and 1 tbsp olive oil and cook until tender. Drain and turn the spaghetti into a bowl. Add the meat mixture and cheese and toss to mix.

5 Arrange aubergine (eggplant) slices over the base and sides of the tin (pan). Add the pasta, then cover with the rest of the aubergine (eggplant). Bake in a preheated oven at 200°C/400°F/ Gas 6 for 40 minutes. Leave to stand for 5 minutes, then invert on to a serving dish. Discard the baking parchment and serve.

Beef & Pasta Bake

Serves 4

INGREDIENTS

900g/2 lb steak, cut into cubes
about 150 ml/^{1}/4 pint/^{5}/8 cup
    beef stock
450g/1 lb dried macaroni
300 ml/^{1}/2 pint/1^1/4 cups
    double (heavy) cream
^{1}/2 tsp garam masala
salt
fresh coriander, to garnish

naan bread, to serve

KORMA PASTE:
60 g/2 oz/^{1}/2 cup blanched
    almonds
6 garlic cloves
2.5 cm/1 inch piece fresh root
    ginger, coarsely chopped
6 tbsp beef stock

1 tsp ground cardamom
4 cloves, crushed
1 tsp cinnamon
2 large onions, chopped
1 tsp coriander seeds
2 tsp ground cumin seeds
pinch of cayenne pepper
6 tbsp of sunflower oil

1 Grind the almonds finely using a pestle and mortar. Blend the ground almonds and the rest of the korma paste ingredients in a food processor or blender to make a very smooth paste.

2 Put the steak in a shallow dish and spoon over the korma paste, turning to coat the steak well. Marinate in the refrigerator for 6 hours.

3 Transfer the steak to a large saucepan, and simmer gently, for 35 minutes, adding a little beef stock if required.

4 Bring a large pan of lightly salted water to the boil. Add the macaroni and cook for 10 minutes, until tender. Drain the pasta and transfer to a deep casserole. Add the steak, double (heavy) cream and garam masala.

5 Bake in a preheated oven at 200°C/400°F/ Gas 6 for 30 minutes. Remove and let stand for 10 minutes. Garnish with fresh coriander and serve with naan bread.

VARIATION

You could also make this dish using diced chicken and chicken stock, instead of steak and beef stock.

Lasagne Verde

Serves 4–6

INGREDIENTS

butter, for greasing	MEAT SAUCE:	300 ml/^{1}/2 pint/1^1/4 cups beef
14 sheets pre-cooked lasagne	25 ml/1 fl oz/^{1}/8 cup olive oil	stock
850 ml/1^1/2 pints/3^3/4 cups	450 g/1 lb/4 cups minced	150 ml/^{1}/4 pint/^{5}/8 cup red
Béchamel Sauce (see page	(ground) beef	wine
166)	1 large onion, chopped	1 tbsp chopped fresh parsley
75 g/3 oz/^{3}/4 cup grated	1 celery stick (stalk), diced	1 tsp chopped fresh marjoram
mozzarella cheese	4 cloves garlic, crushed	1 tsp chopped fresh basil
fresh basil (optional), to	25g/1 oz/^{1}/4 cup plain	2 tbsp tomato purée (paste)
garnish	(all purpose) flour	salt and pepper

1 To make the meat sauce, heat the olive oil in a large frying pan (skillet). Add the minced (ground) beef and fry, stirring frequently, until browned all over. Add the onion, celery and garlic and cook for 3 minutes.

2 Sprinkle over the flour and cook, stirring constantly, for 1 minute. Gradually stir in the stock and red wine. Season well

and add the parsley, marjoram and basil. Bring to the boil, lower the heat and simmer for 35 minutes. Add the tomato purée (paste) and simmer for a further 10 minutes.

3 Lightly grease an ovenproof dish with butter. Arrange sheets of lasagne over the base of the dish, spoon over a layer of meat sauce, then Béchamel Sauce. Place another layer

of lasagne on top and repeat the process twice, finishing with a layer of Béchamel Sauce. Sprinkle over the grated mozzarella cheese.

4 Bake the lasagne in a preheated oven at 190°C/375°F/Gas 5 for 35 minutes, until the top is golden brown and bubbling. Garnish with fresh basil, if liked, and serve immediately.

Pasticcio

Serves 6

INGREDIENTS

250 g/8 oz/2 cups dried fusilli
1 tbsp olive oil, plus extra
   for brushing
4 tbsp double (heavy) cream
mixed salad, to serve

SAUCE:
2 tbsp olive oil
1 onion, thinly sliced
1 red (bell) pepper, cored,
   seeded and chopped

2 garlic cloves, chopped
600 g/1 lb 5 oz/5^{1}/4 cups
   minced (ground) beef
400 g/14 oz can chopped
   tomatoes
125 ml/4 fl oz/^{1}/2 cup dry
   white wine
2 tbsp chopped fresh parsley
60 g/2 oz can anchovies,
   drained and chopped
salt and pepper

TOPPING:
300 ml/^{1}/2 pint/1^{1}/4 cups
   natural yogurt
3 eggs
pinch of freshly grated
   nutmeg
40 g/1^{1}/2 oz/^{1}/2 cup freshly
   grated Parmesan cheese

1 To make the sauce, heat the oil in a frying pan (skillet) and fry the onion and red (bell) pepper for 3 minutes. Add the garlic and cook for 1 minute. Add the beef and cook until browned.

2 Add the tomatoes and wine and bring to the boil. Simmer for 20 minutes, until thickened.

Stir in the parsley, anchovies and seasoning.

3 Bring a pan of salted water to the boil. Add the pasta and oil and cook for 10 minutes, until almost tender. Drain and transfer to a bowl. Stir in the cream.

4 For the topping, beat together the yogurt, eggs and nutmeg.

5 Brush an ovenproof dish with oil. Spoon in half the pasta and cover with half the meat sauce. Repeat, then spread over the topping and sprinkle with cheese.

6 Bake in a preheated oven at 190°C/375°F/ Gas 5 for 25 minutes until golden. Serve with a mixed salad.

Fettuccine with Fillet of Veal & Pink Grapefruit in a Rose Petal Butter Sauce

Serves 4

INGREDIENTS

450 g/1 lb dried fettuccine
7 tbsp olive oil
1 tsp chopped fresh oregano
1 tsp chopped fresh marjoram
170 g/6 oz/³/4 cup butter
450 g/1 lb veal fillet, thinly sliced

150 ml/¹/4 pint/⁵/8 cup rose petal vinegar (see Cook's Tip, below)
150 ml/¹/4 pint/⁵/8 cup fish stock
50 ml/2 fl oz/ ¹/4 cup grapefruit juice
50 ml/2 fl oz/¹/4 cup double (heavy) cream

salt

TO GARNISH:
12 pink grapefruit segments
12 pink peppercorns
rose petals
fresh herb leaves

1 Cook the fettuccine with 1 tbsp of the oil in a pan of salted boiling water for 12 minutes. Drain and transfer to a warm serving dish, sprinkle over 2 tbsp of the olive oil, the oregano and marjoram.

2 Heat 50 g/2 oz/4 tbsp of the butter with the remaining oil in a frying pan (skillet) and cook the veal for 6 minutes. Spoon the veal on top of the pasta.

3 Add the vinegar and fish stock to the pan and boil vigorously until reduced by two thirds. Add the grapefruit juice and cream and simmer for 4 minutes. Dice the remaining butter and add to the pan, whisking until fully incorporated.

4 Pour the sauce around the veal, garnish and serve.

COOK'S TIP

To make rose petal vinegar, infuse the petals of 8 pesticide-free roses in 150 ml/¹/4 pint/⁵/8 cup white wine vinegar for 48 hours.

Neapolitan Veal Cutlets with Mascarpone Cheese & Marille

Serves 4

INGREDIENTS

200 g/7 oz/$^7/_8$ cup butter

4 x 250 g/9 oz veal cutlets, trimmed

1 large onion, sliced

2 apples, peeled, cored and sliced

175 g/6 oz button mushrooms

1 tbsp chopped fresh tarragon

8 black peppercorns

1 tbsp sesame seeds

400 g/14 oz dried marille

100 ml/3$^1/_2$ fl oz/scant $^1/_2$ cup extra virgin olive oil

175 g/6 oz/$^3/_4$ cup mascarpone cheese, broken into small pieces

salt and pepper

2 large beef tomatoes, cut in half

leaves of 1 fresh basil sprig

1 Melt 60 g/2 oz/4 tbsp of the butter in a frying pan (skillet). Gently fry the veal for 5 minutes on each side. Transfer to a dish and keep warm.

2 Fry the onion and apples until golden. Transfer to a dish, top with the veal and keep warm.

3 Fry the mushrooms, tarragon and peppercorns in the remaining butter for 3 minutes. Sprinkle over the sesame seeds.

4 Bring a pan of salted water to the boil. Add the pasta and 1 tbsp of the oil and cook until tender. Drain and transfer to a serving plate.

5 Top the pasta with the cheese and sprinkle over the remaining olive oil. Place the onions, apples and veal cutlets on top of the pasta. Spoon the mushrooms, peppercorns and pan juices on to the cutlets, place the tomatoes and basil leaves around the edge of the plate and place in a preheated oven at 150°C/300°F/Gas 2 for 5 minutes. Season to taste with salt and pepper and serve immediately.

Stir-fried Pork with Pasta & Vegetables

Serves 4

INGREDIENTS
---

3 tbsp sesame oil
350 g/12 oz pork fillet
 (tenderloin), cut into thin
 strips
450 g/1 lb dried taglioni
1 tbsp olive oil
8 shallots, sliced
2 garlic cloves, finely chopped

2.5 cm/1 inch piece fresh root
 ginger, grated
1 fresh green chilli, finely
 chopped
1 red (bell) pepper, cored,
 seeded and thinly sliced
1 green (bell) pepper, cored,
 seeded and thinly sliced

3 courgettes (zucchini), thinly
 sliced
2 tbsp ground almonds
1 tsp ground cinnamon
1 tbsp oyster sauce
60 g/2 oz creamed coconut
 (see Cook's Tip, below),
 grated
salt and pepper

---

1 Heat the sesame oil in a preheated wok. Season the pork and stir-fry for 5 minutes.

2 Bring a pan of salted water to the boil. Add the taglioni and olive oil and cook for 12 minutes. Set aside and keep warm.

3 Add the shallots, garlic, ginger and chilli to the wok and stir-fry for 2 minutes. Add the (bell) peppers and courgettes and stir-fry for 1 minute.

4 Add the ground almonds, cinnamon, oyster sauce and coconut cream to the wok and stir-fry for 1 minute.

5 Drain the taglioni and transfer to a serving dish. Top with the stir-fry and serve immediately.

COOK'S TIP

Creamed coconut is available from Chinese and Asian food stores and some large supermarkets. It is sold in compressed blocks and adds a concentrated coconut flavour to the dish.

Orecchioni with Pork in Cream Sauce, garnished with Quail Eggs

Serves 4

INGREDIENTS

450 g/1 lb pork fillet (tenderloin), thinly sliced
4 tbsp olive oil
225 g/8 oz button mushrooms, sliced

200 ml/7 fl oz/⁷/₈ cup Italian Red Wine Sauce (see page 52)
1 tbsp lemon juice
pinch of saffron

350 g/12 oz/3 cups dried orecchioni
4 tbsp double (heavy) cream
12 quail eggs (see Cook's Tip, below)
salt

1 Pound the slices of pork until wafer thin, then cut into strips.

2 Heat the olive oil in a frying pan (skillet) and stir-fry the pork for 5 minutes, then stir-fry the mushrooms for 2 minutes.

3 Pour over the Italian Red Wine Sauce and simmer for 20 minutes.

4 Meanwhile, bring a large saucepan of lightly salted water to the boil. Add the lemon juice, saffron and orecchioni and cook for 12 minutes, until tender but still firm to the bite. Drain the pasta and keep warm.

5 Stir the cream into the pan with the pork and heat gently for 3 minutes.

6 Boil the quail eggs for 3 minutes, cool them in cold water and remove the shells.

7 Transfer the pasta to a warm serving plate, top with the pork and the sauce and garnish with the eggs. Serve immediately.

COOK'S TIP

In this recipe, the quail eggs are soft-boiled (soft-cooked). As they are very difficult to shell when warm, they should be thoroughly cooled first. Otherwise, they will break up unattractively.

Stuffed Cannelloni

Serves 4

INGREDIENTS

8 dried cannelloni tubes	115 g/4 oz/1¹/₂ cup ricotta	salt and pepper
1 tbsp olive oil	cheese	
25 g/1 oz/¹/₄ cup freshly	25 g/1 oz/¹/₄ cup freshly	SAUCE:
grated Parmesan cheese	grated Parmesan cheese	25 g/1 oz/2 tbsp butter
fresh herb sprigs, to garnish	60 g/2 oz/¹/₄ cup chopped	25 g/1 oz/¹/₄ cup plain
	ham	(all purpose) flour
FILLING:	pinch of freshly grated	300 ml/¹/₂ pint/1¹/₄ cups milk
25 g/1 oz/2 tbsp butter	nutmeg	2 bay leaves
300 g/10¹/₂ oz frozen spinach,	2 tbsp double (heavy) cream	pinch of freshly grated
thawed and chopped	2 eggs, lightly beaten	nutmeg

1 For the filling, melt the butter in a pan and stir-fry the spinach for 2–3 minutes. Remove from the heat and stir in the cheeses and the ham. Season with nutmeg, salt and pepper. Beat in the cream and eggs to make a thick paste.

2 Cook the pasta with the oil in a pan of salted boiling water until tender. Drain and set aside.

3 To make the sauce, melt the butter in a pan. Stir in the flour and cook for 1 minute. Gradually stir in the milk and the bay leaves and simmer for 5 minutes. Add the nutmeg and seasoning. Remove from the heat and discard the bay leaves.

4 Spoon the filling into a piping bag and fill the cannelloni.

5 Spoon a little sauce into the base of an ovenproof dish. Arrange the cannelloni in the dish in a single layer and pour over the remaining sauce. Sprinkle over the Parmesan cheese and bake in a preheated oven at 190°C/375°F/Gas 5 for about 40–45 minutes. Garnish with the fresh herb sprigs and serve immediately.

Tagliatelle with Pumpkin

Serves 4

INGREDIENTS

500 g/1 lb 2 oz pumpkin or
   butternut squash, peeled
   and seeded
3 tbsp olive oil
1 onion, finely chopped
2 garlic cloves, crushed
4–6 tbsp chopped fresh
   parsley

pinch of freshly grated
   nutmeg
about 250 ml/9 fl oz/1¹/₄ cups
   chicken or vegetable stock
115 g/4 oz Parma ham
   (prosciutto)
250 g/9 oz dried tagliatelle

150 ml/¹/₄ pint/⁵/₈ cup double
   (heavy cream)
salt and pepper
freshly grated Parmesan
   cheese, to serve

1 Cut the pumpkin or butternut squash in half and scoop out the seeds. Cut the flesh into 1 cm/¹/₂ inch dice.

2 Heat 2 tbsp of the olive oil in a large saucepan and fry the onion and garlic over a low heat for about 3 minutes, until soft. Add half the parsley and fry for 1 minute.

3 Add the pumpkin or squash pieces and cook for 2–3 minutes. Season to taste with salt, pepper and nutmeg.

4 Add half the stock to the pan, bring to the boil, cover and simmer for 10 minutes, or until the pumpkin or squash is tender, adding more stock if necessary.

5 Add the Parma ham (prosciutto) to the pan and cook, stirring frequently, for 2 minutes.

6 Bring a large pan of lightly salted water to the boil. Add the tagliatelle and the remaining oil and cook for 12 minutes, until tender, but still firm to the bite. Drain and transfer to a warm serving dish.

7 Stir the cream into the pumpkin and ham mixture and heat through. Spoon over the pasta, sprinkle over the remaining parsley and serve immediately.

Aubergine (Eggplant) Cake

Serves 4

INGREDIENTS

1 aubergine (eggplant), thinly sliced
5 tbsp olive oil
250 g/8 oz/2 cups dried fusilli
600 ml/1 pint/2¹/₂ cups Béchamel sauce (see page 166)
90 g/3 oz/³/₄ cup grated Cheddar cheese
butter, for greasing

25 g/1 oz/¹/₃ cup freshly grated Parmesan cheese
salt and pepper

LAMB SAUCE:
1 large onion, sliced
2 celery sticks (stalks), thinly sliced
2 tbsp olive oil

450 g/1 lb minced (ground) lamb
3 tbsp tomato purée (paste)
150 g/5¹/₂ oz bottled sun-dried tomatoes, drained and chopped
1 tsp dried oregano
1 tbsp red wine vinegar
150 ml/¹/₄ pint/⁵/₈ cup chicken stock

1 Sprinkle the aubergine (eggplant) slices with salt and set aside.

2 To make the sauce, fry the onion and celery in the oil for 3–4 minutes. Add the lamb and fry until browned. Stir in the remaining sauce ingredients and boil for 20 minutes.

3 Rinse the aubergine (eggplant) slices, drain and pat dry. Heat 4 tbsp of the oil in a frying pan (skillet). Fry the aubergine (eggplant) slices on each side for 4 minutes. Remove from the pan and drain.

4 Place the fusilli and the remaining oil in a pan of salted boiling water and cook until tender. Drain.

5 Gently heat the Béchamel Sauce. Stir in the Cheddar and then stir half of the cheese sauce into the fusilli.

6 Make layers of fusilli, lamb sauce and aubergine (eggplant) in a greased dish. Top with the remaining cheese sauce. Sprinkle with Parmesan and bake in a preheated oven at 190°C/375°F/Gas 5 for 25 minutes. Serve hot or cold.

Wholemeal (Whole wheat) Spaghetti with Suprêmes of Chicken Nell Gwyn

Serves 4

INGREDIENTS

25 ml/1 fl oz/^{1}/8 cup rapeseed oil

3 tbsp olive oil

4 x 225 g/8 oz chicken suprêmes

150 ml/^{1}/4 pint/^{5}/8 cup orange brandy

15 g/^{1}/2 oz/2 tbsp plain (all purpose) flour

150 ml/^{1}/4 pint/^{5}/8 cup freshly squeezed orange juice

25 g/1 oz courgette (zucchini), cut into matchstick strips

25 g/1 oz red (bell) pepper, cut into matchstick strips

25 g/1 oz leek, finely shredded

400 g/14 oz dried wholemeal (whole wheat) spaghetti

3 large oranges, peeled and cut into segments

rind of 1 orange, cut into very fine strips

2 tbsp chopped fresh tarragon

150 ml/^{1}/4 pint/^{5}/8 cup fromage frais or ricotta cheese

salt and pepper

1 Heat the rapeseed oil and 1 tbsp of the olive oil in a frying pan (skillet). Add the chicken and cook quickly until golden brown. Add the orange brandy and cook for 3 minutes. Sprinkle over the flour and cook for 2 minutes.

2 Lower the heat and add the orange juice, courgette (zucchini), (bell) pepper and leek and season. Simmer for 5 minutes until the sauce has thickened.

3 Meanwhile, bring a pan of salted water to the boil. Add the spaghetti and 1 tbsp of the olive oil and cook for 10 minutes. Drain, transfer to a serving dish and drizzle over the remaining oil.

4 Add half the orange segments, half the orange rind, the tarragon and fromage frais or ricotta cheese to the sauce in the pan and cook for 3 minutes.

5 Place the chicken on top of the pasta, pour over a little sauce, garnish with orange segments and rind. Serve immediately.

Chicken & Wild Mushroom Lasagne

Serves 4

INGREDIENTS

butter, for greasing
14 sheets pre-cooked lasagne
850 ml/1¹/₂ pints/3³/₄ cups
    Béchamel Sauce (see page
    166)
75 g/3 oz/1 cup grated
    Parmesan cheese

CHICKEN & WILD MUSHROOM
    SAUCE:
2 tbsp olive oil
2 garlic cloves, crushed
1 large onion, finely chopped
225 g/8 oz wild mushrooms,
    sliced
300 g/10¹/₂ oz/2¹/₂ cups
    minced (ground) chicken
80 g/3 oz chicken livers,
    finely chopped

115 g/4 oz Parma ham
    (prosciutto), diced
150 ml/¹/₄ pint/⁵/₈ cup
    Marsala
285g/10 oz can chopped
    tomatoes
1 tbsp chopped fresh basil
    leaves
2 tbsp tomato purée (paste)
salt and pepper

1 To make the sauce, heat the olive oil in a large saucepan. Add the garlic, onion and mushrooms and cook for 6 minutes.

2 Add the minced (ground) chicken, chicken livers and Parma ham (prosciutto) and cook for 12 minutes, until the meat has browned.

3 Stir the Marsala, tomatoes, basil and tomato purée (paste) into the pan and cook for 4 minutes. Season, cover and simmer for 30 minutes. Stir and simmer for a further 15 minutes.

4 Arrange the lasagne over the base of a greased ovenproof dish, spoon over a layer of chicken and wild mushroom sauce, then a layer of Béchamel Sauce. Place another layer of lasagne on top and repeat the process twice, finishing with a layer of Béchamel Sauce. Sprinkle over the grated cheese and bake in a preheated oven at 190°C/375°F/Gas 5 for 35 minutes until golden brown. Serve immediately.

Tagliatelle with Chicken Sauce

Serves 4

INGREDIENTS

250 g/9 oz fresh green
    tagliatelle
1 tbsp olive oil
fresh basil leaves, to garnish
salt

TOMATO SAUCE:
2 tbsp olive oil
1 small onion, chopped
1 garlic clove, chopped

400 g/14 oz can chopped
    tomatoes
2 tbsp chopped fresh parsley
1 tsp dried oregano
2 bay leaves
2 tbsp tomato purée (paste)
1 tsp sugar
salt and pepper

CHICKEN SAUCE:
60 g/2 oz/4 tbsp unsalted
    butter
400 g/14 oz boned chicken
    breasts, skinned and cut
    into thin strips
90 g/3 oz/^{3}/4 cup blanched
    almonds
300 ml/^{1}/2 pint/1^1/4 cups
    double (heavy) cream
salt and pepper

1 To make the tomato sauce, heat the oil and fry the onion until translucent. Add the garlic and fry for 1 minute. Stir in the tomatoes, herbs, tomato purée (paste), sugar and seasoning to taste. Bring to the boil and simmer for 15–20 minutes, until reduced by half. Remove from the heat and discard the bay leaves.

2 To make the chicken sauce, melt the butter in a frying pan (skillet) and stir-fry the chicken and almonds for 5–6 minutes, until the chicken is cooked.

3 Meanwhile, bring the cream to the boil over a low heat for about 10 minutes, until reduced by half. Pour the cream over the chicken and almonds,

stir and season to taste. Set aside and keep warm.

4 Bring a pan of salted water to the boil. Add the tagliatelle and olive oil and cook until tender. Drain and transfer to a warm serving dish. Spoon over the tomato sauce and arrange the chicken sauce on top. Garnish with the basil leaves and serve.

Mustard Baked Chicken with Pasta Shells

Serves 4

INGREDIENTS

8 chicken pieces
   (about 115 g/4 oz each)
60g/2 oz/4 tbsp butter, melted
4 tbsp mild mustard (see
   Cook's Tip)

2 tbsp lemon juice
1 tbsp brown sugar
1 tsp paprika
3 tbsp poppy seeds
400 g/14 oz fresh pasta shells

1 tbsp olive oil
salt and pepper

1 Arrange the chicken, smooth side down, in an ovenproof dish.

2 Combine the butter, mustard, lemon juice, sugar, paprika and salt and pepper. Brush the mixture over the upper surfaces of the chicken pieces and bake in a preheated oven at 200°C/400°F/Gas 6 for 15 minutes.

3 Remove the dish from the oven and turn over the chicken pieces. Coat the upper surfaces of the chicken with the remaining mustard mixture, sprinkle with poppy seeds and return to the oven for a further 15 minutes.

4 Meanwhile, bring a large pan of lightly salted water to the boil. Add the pasta shells and olive oil and cook until tender, but still firm to the bite.

5 Drain the pasta and arrange on a warmed serving dish. Top with the chicken, pour over the sauce and serve immediately.

COOK'S TIP

Dijon is the type of mustard most often used in cooking, as it has a clean and only mildly spicy flavour. German mustard has a sweet-sour taste, with Bavarian mustard being slightly sweeter. American mustard is mild and sweet.

Tortellini

Serves 4

INGREDIENTS

115 g/4 oz boned chicken breast, skinned	pinch of ground allspice	SAUCE:
60 g/2 oz Parma ham (prosciutto)	1 egg, beaten	300 ml/^{1}/2 pint/1^1/4 cups single (light) cream
40 g/1^1/2 oz cooked spinach, well drained	450 g/1 lb Basic Pasta Dough (see page 4)	2 garlic cloves, crushed
1 tbsp finely chopped onion	salt and pepper	115 g/4 oz button mushrooms, thinly sliced
2 tbsp freshly grated Parmesan cheese	2 tbsp chopped fresh parsley, to garnish	4 tbsp freshly grated Parmesan cheese

1 Bring a pan of seasoned water to the boil. Add the chicken and poach for 10 minutes. Cool slightly, then process in a food processor, with the Parma ham (prosciutto), spinach and onion until finely chopped. Stir in the Parmesan cheese, allspice and egg and season to taste.

2 Thinly roll out the pasta dough and cut into 5 cm/2 inch rounds.

3 Place ½ tsp of the filling in the centre of each round. Fold the pieces in half and press the edges to seal. Then wrap each piece around your index finger, cross over the ends and curl the rest of the dough backwards to make a navel shape.

4 Bring a pan of salted water to the boil. Add the tortellini, bring back to the boil and cook for

5 minutes. Drain and transfer to a serving dish.

5 To make the sauce, bring the cream and garlic to the boil then simmer for 3 minutes. Add the mushrooms and half the cheese, season and simmer for 2–3 minutes. Pour the sauce over the tortellini. Sprinkle over the remaining Parmesan, garnish with the parsley and serve.

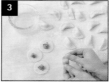

Chicken Suprêmes Filled with Tiger Prawns (Shrimp) on a Bed of Pasta

Serves 4

INGREDIENTS

4 x 200 g/7 oz chicken
    suprêmes, trimmed
115 g/4 oz large spinach leaves,
    trimmed and blanched in
    hot salted water
4 slices of Parma ham
    (prosciutto)

12–16 raw tiger prawns
    (shrimp), shelled and
    deveined
450g/1 lb dried tagliatelle
1 tbsp olive oil
60 g/2 oz/4 tbsp butter, plus
    extra for greasing

3 leeks, shredded
1 large carrot, grated
150 ml/¼ pint/⁵⁄₈ cup
    thick mayonnaise
2 large cooked beetroot (beet)
salt

1 Place each suprême between 2 pieces of baking parchment and pound to flatten.

2 Divide half the spinach between the suprêmes, add a slice of ham to each and top with spinach. Place 3–4 prawns (shrimp) on top. Roll up each suprême to form a parcel. Wrap each parcel in greased foil, place on a baking (cookie) sheet and bake in a preheated oven at 200°C/400°F/Gas 6 for 20 minutes.

3 Cook the pasta with the oil in salted boiling water until tender. Drain and transfer to a warm dish.

4 Melt the butter and fry the leeks and carrot for 3 minutes. Transfer to the centre of the pasta.

5 Work the mayonnaise and 1 beetroot (beet) in a food processor until smooth. Rub through a strainer and pour around the pasta and vegetables.

6 Cut the remaining beetroot (beet) into diamond shapes and place them around the mayonnaise. Remove the foil from the chicken and cut the suprêmes into thin slices. Arrange the slices on top of the vegetables and pasta, and serve.

Chicken & Lobster on a Bed of Penne

Serves 6

INGREDIENTS

butter, for greasing
6 chicken breasts
450 g/1 lb dried penne rigate
6 tbsp extra virgin olive oil
90 g/3 oz/1 cup freshly grated
   Parmesan cheese

salt
fresh herbs, to garnish

FILLING:
115 g/4 oz lobster meat,
   chopped

2 shallots, very finely chopped
2 figs, chopped
1 tbsp Marsala
2 tbsp breadcrumbs
1 large egg, beaten
salt and pepper

1 Grease 6 pieces of foil large enough to enclose each chicken breast and lightly grease a baking (cookie) sheet.

2 Place all of the filling ingredients into a mixing bowl and blend together thoroughly with a spoon.

3 Cut a pocket in each chicken breast with a sharp knife and fill with the lobster mixture. Wrap each chicken breast in foil, place the parcels on the greased baking (cookie) sheet and bake in a preheated oven at 200°C/400°F/Gas 6 for 30 minutes.

4 Meanwhile, bring a large pan of lightly salted water to the boil. Add the pasta and 1 tbsp of the olive oil and cook for about 10 minutes, or until tender but still firm to the bite. Drain the pasta thoroughly and transfer to a large serving plate. Sprinkle over the remaining olive oil and the grated Parmesan cheese, set aside and keep warm.

5 Carefully remove the foil from around the chicken breasts. Slice the breasts very thinly, arrange over the pasta. Garnish with fresh herbs and serve immediately.

COOK'S TIP

The cut of chicken known as suprême consists of the breast and wing. It is always skinned.

Chicken with Green Olives & Pasta

Serves 4

INGREDIENTS

4 chicken breasts, part boned
3 tbsp olive oil
25 g/1 oz/2 tbsp butter
1 large onion, finely chopped
2 garlic cloves, crushed
2 red, yellow or green (bell)
   peppers, cored, seeded and
   cut into large pieces

250 g/9 oz button
   mushrooms, sliced or
   quartered
175 g/6 oz tomatoes, skinned
   and halved
150 ml/$\frac{1}{4}$ pint/$\frac{5}{8}$ cup dry
   white wine

175 g/6 oz/1$\frac{1}{2}$ cups stoned
   (pitted) green olives
4–6 tbsp double (heavy) cream
400 g/14 oz dried pasta
salt and pepper
chopped parsley, to garnish

1 Fry the chicken breasts in 2 tbsp of the oil and the butter until golden brown. Remove the chicken from the pan.

2 Add the onion and garlic to the pan and fry until beginning to soften. Add the (bell) peppers and mushrooms and cook for 2–3 minutes. Add the tomatoes and seasoning. Transfer the vegetables to a casserole with the chicken.

3 Add the wine to the pan and bring to the boil. Pour the wine over the chicken. Cover and cook in a preheated oven at 180°C/350°F/Gas 4 for 50 minutes.

4 Mix the olives into the casserole. Pour in the cream, cover and return to the oven for 10–20 minutes.

5 Meanwhile, bring a large pan of lightly salted water to the boil. Add the pasta and the remaining oil and cook until tender, but still firm to the bite. Drain the pasta well and transfer to a serving dish.

6 Arrange the chicken on top of the pasta, spoon over the sauce, garnish with the parsley and serve immediately. Alternatively, place the pasta in a large serving bowl and serve separately.

Sliced Breast of Duckling with Linguine

Serves 4

INGREDIENTS

4 x 275 g/10^{1}/$_{2}$ oz boned
   breasts of duckling
25 g/1 oz/2 tbsp butter
50 g/2 oz/3^{3}/$_{8}$ cup finely
   chopped carrots
50 g/2 oz/4 tbsp finely
   chopped shallots
1 tbsp lemon juice

150 ml/^{1}/$_{4}$ pint/^{5}/$_{8}$ cup meat
   stock
4 tbsp clear honey
115 g/4 oz/^{3}/$_{4}$ cup fresh or
   thawed frozen raspberries
25 g/1 oz/^{1}/$_{4}$ cup plain (all
   purpose) flour
1 tbsp Worcestershire sauce

400 g/14 oz fresh linguine
1 tbsp olive oil
salt and pepper

TO GARNISH:
fresh raspberries
fresh sprig of flat-leaf parsley

1 Trim and score the duck breasts and season well. Melt the butter in a frying pan (skillet) and fry the duck breasts until lightly coloured.

2 Add the carrots, shallots, lemon juice and half the meat stock and simmer for 1 minute. Stir in half the honey and half the raspberries. Stir in half

the flour and cook for 3 minutes. Add the pepper and Worcestershire sauce.

3 Stir in the remaining stock and cook for 1 minute. Stir in the remaining honey, raspberries and flour. Cook for a further 3 minutes.

4 Remove the duck from the pan, but continue simmering the sauce.

5 Bring a large pan of salted water to the boil. Add the linguine and olive oil and cook until tender. Drain and divide between 4 plates.

6 Slice the duck breast lengthways into 5 mm/^{1}/$_{4}$ inch thick pieces. Pour a little sauce over the pasta and arrange the sliced duck in a fan shape on top. Garnish and serve.

Rigatoni & Pesto Baked Partridge

Serves 4

INGREDIENTS

8 partridge pieces
 (about 115 g/4 oz each)
60 g/2 oz/4 tbsp butter, melted
4 tbsp Dijon mustard
2 tbsp lime juice

1 tbsp brown sugar
6 tbsp Pesto Sauce (see
 page 12)
450 g/1 lb dried rigatoni
1 tbsp olive oil

115 g/4 oz/1¹/₃ cups freshly
 grated Parmesan cheese
salt and pepper

1 Arrange the partridge pieces, smooth side down, in a single layer in a large, ovenproof dish.

2 Mix together the butter, Dijon mustard, lime juice and brown sugar in a bowl. Season to taste. Brush the mixture over the upper surfaces of the partridge pieces and bake in a preheated oven at 200°C/400°F/Gas 6 for 15 minutes.

3 Remove the dish from the oven and coat the partridge pieces with 3 tbsp of the Pesto Sauce. Return to the oven and bake for a further 12 minutes.

4 Remove the dish from the oven and carefully turn over the partridge pieces. Coat the top of the partridges with the remaining mustard mixture and return to the oven for a further 10 minutes.

5 Meanwhile, bring a large saucepan of lightly salted water to the boil. Add the rigatoni and olive oil and cook for about 10 minutes until tender, but still firm to the bite. Drain and transfer to a serving dish. Toss the pasta with the remaining Pesto Sauce and the Parmesan.

6 Arrange the pieces of partridge on the serving dish with the rigatoni, pour over the cooking juices and serve immediately.

VARIATION

You could also prepare young pheasant in the same way.

Breast of Pheasant Lasagne with Baby Onions & Green Peas

Serves 4

INGREDIENTS

butter, for greasing
14 sheets pre-cooked lasagne
850 ml/1^1/3 pints/3^3/4 cups
   Béchamel Sauce (see page
   166)
75 g/3 oz/^{3}/4 cup grated
   mozzarella cheese

FILLING:
225 g/8 oz pork fat, diced
60 g/2 oz/2 tbsp butter
16 small onions
8 large pheasant breasts,
   thinly sliced

25 g/1 oz/^{1}/4 cup plain
   (all purpose) flour
600 ml/1 pint/2^1/2 cups
   chicken stock
bouquet garni
450 g/1 lb fresh peas, shelled
salt and pepper

1 Put the pork fat into a pan of boiling, salted water and simmer for 3 minutes, drain and pat dry.

2 Fry the pork fat and onions in the butter until lightly browned. Remove from the pan.

3 Add the pheasant to the pan and cook over a low heat until browned all over. Transfer to an ovenproof dish.

4 Stir the flour into the pan and cook until brown, then blend in the stock. Pour over the pheasant, add the bouquet garni and cook in a preheated oven at 200°C/400°F/Gas 6 for 5 minutes.

5 Remove the bouquet garni. Add the onions, pork fat and peas and return to the oven for 10 minutes.

6 Mince the pheasant breasts and pork in a food processor.

7 Lower the oven to 190°C/375°F/Gas 5. Make layers of lasagne, pheasant sauce and Béchamel Sauce in an ovenproof dish, ending with Béchamel sauce. Sprinkle over the cheese and bake in the oven for 30 minutes. Serve surrounded by the peas and onions.

Fish & Seafood

Pasta is a natural partner for fish
and seafood. Both are cooked quickly to
preserve their flavour and texture,
they are packed full of nutritional goodness
and the varieties available are almost infinite.
The superb recipes in this chapter demonstrate
the full range of these qualities. For a quick, easy
and satisfying supper, try Spaghetti al Tonno,
Casserole of Fusilli & Smoked Haddock with
Egg Sauce, Seafood Lasagne or Macaroni
and Prawn (Shrimp) Bake. More unusual
and sophisticated dishes include Sea Bass
with Olive Sauce on a Bed of Macaroni,
Poached Salmon Steaks with Penne,
Farfallini Buttered Lobster and Baked
Scallops with Pasta in Shells. There are
dishes to suit all tastes – freshwater and
sea fish, shellfish and other seafood – and
to suit all pockets. All are easy to
make; the only problem is choosing
which one to cook next.

Cannelloni Filetti di Sogliola

Serves 6

INGREDIENTS

12 small fillets of sole (about 115 g/4 oz each)	4 shallots, finely chopped	2 tbsp double (heavy) cream
150 ml/^{1}/4 pint/^{5}/8 cup red wine	115 g/4 oz tomatoes, chopped	6 dried cannelloni tubes
90 g/3 oz/6 tbsp butter	2 tbsp tomato purée (paste)	175 g/6 oz cooked, peeled prawns (shrimp), preferably freshwater
115 g/4 oz/3^7/8 cups sliced button mushrooms	60 g/2 oz/^{1}/2 cup plain (all purpose) flour, sifted	salt and pepper
	150 ml/^{1}/4 pint/^{5}/8 cup of warm milk	1 fresh dill sprig, to garnish

1 Brush the fillets with a little wine. Season and roll up, skin side inwards. Secure with a skewer or cocktail stick (toothpick).

2 Arrange the fish rolls in a single layer in a large frying pan (skillet), add the remaining red wine and poach for 4 minutes. Remove from the pan and reserve the cooking liquid.

3 Melt the butter in another pan. Fry the mushrooms and shallots for 2 minutes, then add the tomatoes and tomato purée (paste). Season the flour and stir it into the pan. Stir in the reserved cooking liquid and half the milk. Cook over a low heat, stirring, for 4 minutes. Remove from the heat and stir in the cream.

4 Bring a pan of salted water to the boil. Add the cannelloni and cook for 8 minutes, until tender but still firm to the bite. Drain and set aside to cool.

5 Remove the skewers or cocktail sticks from the fish rolls. Put 2 sole fillets into each cannelloni tube with 3–4 prawns (shrimp) and a little red wine sauce. Arrange the cannelloni in an ovenproof dish, pour over the sauce and bake in a preheated oven at 200°C/ 400°F/ Gas 6 for 20 minutes.

6 Serve the cannelloni with the red wine sauce, garnished with a sprig of dill.

Sea Bass with Olive Sauce on a Bed of Macaroni

Serves 4

INGREDIENTS

450 g/1 lb dried macaroni
1 tbsp olive oil
8 x 115 g/4 oz sea bass
    medallions

TO GARNISH:
lemon slices
shredded leek
shredded carrot

SAUCE:
25 g/1 oz/2 tbsp butter
4 shallots, chopped
2 tbsp capers
175 g/6 oz/1^1/$_2$ cups stoned
    (pitted) green olives,
    chopped
4 tbsp balsamic vinegar

300 ml/^{1}/$_2$ pint/1^1/$_4$ cups fish
    stock
300 ml/^{1}/$_2$ pint/1^1/$_4$ cups
    double (heavy) cream
juice of 1 lemon
salt and pepper

1 For the sauce, melt the butter in a frying pan (skillet) and cook the shallots for 4 minutes. Add the capers and olives and cook for 3 minutes.

2 Stir in the balsamic vinegar and fish stock, bring to the boil and reduce by half. Stir in the cream and reduce again by half. Season to taste and stir in the lemon juice. Remove the pan from the heat, set aside and keep warm.

3 Bring a large pan of lightly salted water to the boil. Add the pasta and olive oil and cook for about 12 minutes, until tender but still firm to the bite.

4 Lightly grill (broil) the sea bass medallions for 3–4 minutes on each side, until cooked through, but still moist and delicate.

5 Drain the pasta and transfer to individual serving dishes. Top the pasta with the fish medallions and pour over the olive sauce. Garnish with lemon slices, shredded leek and shredded carrot and serve.

Spaghetti alla Bucaniera

Serves 4

INGREDIENTS

90 g/3 oz/³/₄ cup plain (all purpose) flour
450 g/1 lb brill or sole fillets, skinned and chopped
450 g/1 lb hake fillets, skinned and chopped
90 g/3 oz/6 tbsp butter
4 shallots, finely chopped

2 garlic cloves, crushed
1 carrot, diced
1 leek, finely chopped
300 ml/¹/₂ pint/1¹/₄ cups dry (hard) cider
300 ml/¹/₂ pint/¹/₄ cups medium sweet cider
1 tbsp tarragon vinegar

2 tsp anchovy essence (extract)
450 g/1 lb dried spaghetti
1 tbsp olive oil
salt and pepper
chopped fresh parsley, to garnish
crusty brown bread, to serve

1 Season the flour with salt and pepper. Sprinkle 25 g/1 oz/¼ cup of the seasoned flour on to a shallow plate. Press the fish pieces into the seasoned flour to coat thoroughly.

2 Melt the butter in a flameproof casserole. Add the fish fillets, shallots, garlic, carrot and leek and cook over a low heat, stirring frequently, for about 10 minutes.

3 Sprinkle over the remaining seasoned flour and cook, stirring constantly, for 2 minutes. Gradually stir in the cider, tarragon vinegar and anchovy essence (extract). Bring to the boil and simmer over a low heat for 35 minutes. Alternatively, bake in a preheated oven at 180°C/350°F/Gas 4 for 30 minutes.

4 About 15 minutes before the end of the

cooking time, bring a pan of lightly salted water to the boil. Add the spaghetti and olive oil and cook for 12 minutes, or until tender but still firm to the bite. Drain the pasta and transfer to a serving dish.

5 Arrange the fish on top of the spaghetti and pour over the sauce. Garnish with chopped parsley and serve immediately with warm, crusty brown bread.

Steamed Pasta Pudding

Serves 4

INGREDIENTS

115 g/4 oz/1 cup dried short-cut macaroni or other short pasta	2–3 fresh parsley sprigs	60 g/2 oz/²/₃ cup freshly grated Parmesan cheese
1 tbsp olive oil	6 black peppercorns	salt and pepper
15 g/¹/₂ oz/1 tbsp butter, plus extra for greasing	125 ml/4 fl oz/¹/₂ cup double (heavy) cream	fresh dill or parsley sprigs, to garnish
450 g/1 lb white fish fillets, such as cod or haddock	2 eggs, separated	tomato sauce (see page 54), to serve
	2 tbsp chopped fresh dill or parsley	
	pinch of freshly grated nutmeg	

1 Bring a pan of salted water to the boil. Add the pasta and olive oil and cook until tender. Drain, return to the pan, add the butter, cover and keep warm.

2 Place the fish, parsley, peppercorns and enough water to cover in a frying pan (skillet). Bring to the boil, cover and simmer for 10 minutes. Remove the fish and reserve the cooking liquid.

3 Skin the fish and cut into bite-size pieces. Combine the cream, egg yolks, chopped dill or parsley, nutmeg and cheese and mix with the pasta in a bowl. Carefully spoon in the fish. Add enough of the reserved cooking liquid to make a moist, but firm mixture. Whisk the egg whites until stiff, then fold them into the mixture.

4 Grease a heatproof bowl and spoon the

fish mixture to within 4 cm/1½ inches of the rim. Cover with greased greaseproof (baking) paper and foil and tie securely with string.

5 Stand the bowl on a trivet in a saucepan. Add boiling water to reach halfway up the sides. Cover and steam for 1½ hours. Invert the pudding on to a serving plate. Garnish and serve with the tomato sauce.

Red Mullet Fillets with Orecchiette, Amaretto & Orange Sauce

Serves 4

INGREDIENTS

90 g/3 oz/3³/4 cup plain (all purpose) flour
8 red mullet fillets
25 g/1 oz/2 tbsp butter
150 ml/¹/4 pint/⁵/8 cup fish stock
1 tbsp crushed almonds
1 tsp pink peppercorns

1 orange, peeled and cut into segments
1 tbsp orange liqueur
grated rind of 1 orange
450 g/1 lb dried orecchiette
1 tbsp olive oil
150 ml/¹/4 pint/⁵/8 cup double (heavy) cream

4 tbsp amaretto
salt and pepper

TO GARNISH:
2 tbsp snipped fresh chives
1 tbsp toasted almonds

1 Season the flour and sprinkle into a shallow bowl. Press the fish fillets into the flour to coat. Melt the butter in a frying pan (skillet) and fry the fish over a low heat for 3 minutes, until browned.

2 Add the fish stock to the pan and cook for 4 minutes. Carefully remove the fish, cover with foil and keep warm.

3 Add the almonds, pink peppercorns, half the orange, the orange liqueur and orange rind to the pan. Simmer until the liquid has reduced by half.

4 Meanwhile, bring a large saucepan of lightly salted water to the boil. Add the orecchiette and olive oil and cook for 15 minutes, until tender but still firm to the bite.

5 Season the sauce and stir in the cream and amaretto. Cook for 2 minutes. Coat the fish with the sauce in the pan.

6 Drain the pasta and transfer to a serving dish. Top with the fish fillets and their sauce. Garnish with the remaining orange segments, the chives and toasted almonds. Serve.

Vermicelli with Fillets of Red Mullet

Serves 4

INGREDIENTS
---

1 kg/2¼ lb red mullet fillets
300 ml/½ pint/1¼ cups dry
  white wine
4 shallots, finely chopped
1 garlic clove, crushed
3 tbsp mixed fresh herbs
finely grated rind and juice of
  1 lemon

pinch of freshly grated
  nutmeg
3 anchovy fillets, roughly
  chopped
2 tbsp double (heavy) cream
1 tsp cornflour (cornstarch)
450 g/1 lb dried vermicelli
1 tbsp olive oil

salt and pepper

TO GARNISH:
1 fresh mint sprig
lemon slices
lemon rind

1 Put the red mullet fillets in a large casserole. Pour over the wine and add the shallots, garlic, herbs, lemon rind and juice, nutmeg and anchovies. Season with salt and pepper to taste. Cover and bake in a preheated oven at 180°C/350°F/Gas 4 for 35 minutes.

2 Carefully transfer the mullet and herbs to a warm dish. Set aside and keep warm.

3 Pour the cooking liquid into a pan and bring to the boil. Simmer for 25 minutes, until reduced by half. Mix the cream and cornflour (cornstarch) and stir into the sauce to thicken.

4 Bring a pan of salted water to the boil. Add the vermicelli and olive oil and cook until tender, but still firm to the bite. Drain the pasta and transfer to a warm serving dish.

5 Discard the herbs before arranging the red mullet fillets on top of the vermicelli; pour over the sauce. Garnish with a fresh mint sprig, slices of lemon and strips of lemon rind. Serve immediately.

COOK'S TIP

The best red mullet is sometimes called golden mullet, although it is bright red in colour.

Spaghetti al Tonno

Serves 4

INGREDIENTS

200 g/7 oz can tuna, drained
60 g/2 oz can anchovies,
    drained
250 ml/9 fl oz/1^{1}/8 cups
    olive oil

60 g/2 oz/1 cup roughly
    chopped flat leaf parsley,
    plus extra to garnish
150 ml/^{1}/4 pint/^{5}/8 cup crème
    fraîche

450 g/1 lb dried spaghetti
25 g/1 oz/2 tbsp butter
salt and pepper
black olives, to garnish
crusty bread, to serve

1 Remove any bones from the tuna. Put the tuna into a food processor or blender, together with the anchovies, 225 ml/ 8 fl oz/1 cup of the olive oil and the flat leaf parsley. Process until smooth.

2 Spoon the crème fraîche into the food processor or blender and process again for a few seconds to blend thoroughly. Season to taste.

3 Bring a large pan of lightly salted water to the boil. Add the spaghetti

and the remaining olive oil and cook until tender, but still firm to the bite.

4 Drain the spaghetti, return to the pan and place over a medium heat. Add the butter and toss well to coat. Spoon in the sauce and quickly toss into the spaghetti, using 2 forks.

5 Remove the pan from the heat and divide the spaghetti between 4 warm individual serving plates. Garnish with olives and parsley and serve with warm, crusty bread.

VARIATION

If liked, you could add 1–2 garlic cloves to the sauce, substitute 25 g/ 1 oz/^{1}/2 cup chopped fresh basil for half the parsley and garnish with capers instead of black olives.

Casserole of Fusilli & Smoked Haddock with Egg Sauce

Serves 4

INGREDIENTS

25 g/1 oz/2 tbsp butter, plus extra for greasing
450 g/1 lb smoked haddock fillets, cut into 4 slices
600 ml/1 pint/2¹/₂ cups milk
25 g/1 oz/¹/₄ cup plain (all purpose) flour

pinch of freshly grated nutmeg
3 tbsp double (heavy) cream
1 tbsp chopped fresh parsley, plus extra to garnish
2 eggs, hard boiled (hard cooked) and mashed

450 g/1 lb/4 cups dried fusilli
1 tbsp lemon juice
salt and pepper
boiled new potatoes and beetroot (beet), to serve

1 Grease a casserole with butter. Put the haddock in the casserole and pour over the milk. Bake in a preheated oven at 200°C/400°G/Gas 6 for 15 minutes. Carefully pour the cooking liquid into a jug (pitcher) without breaking up the fish.

2 Melt the butter in a saucepan and stir in the flour. Gradually whisk in the reserved cooking liquid. Season with salt, pepper and nutmeg. Stir in the cream, parsley and mashed eggs and cook for 2 minutes.

3 Meanwhile, bring a large saucepan of salted water to the boil. Add the fusilli and lemon juice and cook until tender, but still firm to the bite.

4 Drain the pasta and tip it over the fish. Top with the sauce and return to the oven for 10 minutes.

5 Garnish and serve the casserole with boiled new potatoes and beetroot (beet).

VARIATION

You can use any type of dried pasta for this casserole. Try penne, conchiglie or rigatoni.

Ravioli of Lemon Sole & Haddock

Serves 4

INGREDIENTS

450 g/1 lb lemon sole fillets,
  skinned
450 g/1 lb haddock fillets,
  skinned
3 eggs beaten
450 g/1 lb cooked potato
  gnocchi (see page 58)

175 g/6 oz/3 cups fresh
  breadcrumbs
50 ml/2 fl oz/^{1}/4 cup double
  (heavy) cream
450 g/1 lb Basic Pasta Dough
  (see page 4)

300 ml/^{1}/2 pint/1^1/4 cups
  Italian Red Wine Sauce
  (see page 52)
60 g/2 oz/^{2}/3 cup freshly
  grated Parmesan cheese
salt and pepper

1 Flake the fish fillets in a large mixing bowl.

2 Mix the eggs, cooked potato gnocchi, breadcrumbs and cream in a bowl until combined. Add the fish and season the mixture to taste.

3 Roll out the pasta dough on to a lightly floured surface and cut out 7.5 cm/3 inch rounds.

4 Place a spoonful of the fish stuffing on each round. Dampen the edges slightly and fold the pasta rounds over, pressing together to seal.

5 Bring a large saucepan of lightly salted water to the boil. Add the ravioli and cook for 15 minutes.

6 Drain the ravioli, using a slotted spoon, and transfer to a large serving dish. Pour over the Italian Red Wine Sauce, sprinkle over the Parmesan cheese and serve immediately.

COOK'S TIP

For square ravioli, divide the dough into two. Wrap half in cling film and thinly roll out the other half. Cover with a clean, damp tea towel while rolling the remaining dough. Spoon the filling at regular intervals and brush the gaps with water or beaten egg. Cover with the second sheet of dough and press firmly between the filling to seal and expel any air. Cut out the shapes with a knife.

Poached Salmon Steaks with Penne

Serves 4

INGREDIENTS
---

4 x 275 g/10 oz fresh salmon
  steaks
60 g/2 oz/4 tbsp butter
175 ml/6 fl oz/³/4 cup dry
  white wine
sea salt
8 peppercorns
fresh dill sprig
fresh tarragon sprig

1 lemon, sliced
450 g/1 lb dried penne
2 tbsp olive oil
lemon slices and fresh
  watercress, to garnish

LEMON & WATERCRESS
  SAUCE:
.25 g/1 oz/2 tbsp butter

25 g/1 oz/¹/4 cup plain (all
  purpose) flour
150 ml/¹/4 pint/⁵/8 cup warm
  milk
juice and finely grated rind of
  2 lemons
60 g/2 oz watercress, chopped
salt and pepper

---

1 Put the salmon in a large, non-stick pan. Add the butter, wine, a pinch of sea salt, the peppercorns, dill, tarragon and lemon. Cover, bring to the boil, and simmer for 10 minutes.

2 Using a slotted spoon, carefully remove the salmon. Strain and reserve the cooking liquid. Remove and discard the salmon skin and centre bones. Place on a warm dish, cover and keep warm.

3 Bring a pan of salted water to the boil. Add the penne and 1 tbsp of oil and cook for 12 minutes. Drain and sprinkle over the remaining oil. Place on a serving dish, top with the salmon and keep warm.

4 To make the sauce, melt the butter and stir in the flour for 2 minutes.

Stir in the milk and about 7 tbsp of the reserved cooking liquid. Add the lemon juice and rind and cook, stirring, for a further 10 minutes.

5 Stir in the watercress and seasoning.

6 Pour the sauce over the salmon and penne, garnish with slices of lemon and fresh watercress and serve immediately.

Spaghetti with Smoked Salmon

Serves 4

INGREDIENTS

450 g/1 lb dried buckwheat
    spaghetti
2 tbsp olive oil
90 g/3 oz/$^1/_2$ cup crumbled
    feta cheese
salt

fresh coriander (cilantro) or
    parsley leaves, to garnish

SAUCE:
300 ml/$^1/_2$ pint/$1^1/_4$ cups
    double (heavy) cream
150 ml/$^1/_4$ pint/$^5/_8$ cup whisky
    or brandy

125 g/4$^1/_2$ oz smoked salmon
pinch of cayenne pepper
black pepper
2 tbsp chopped fresh coriander
    (cilantro) or parsley

1 Bring a large pan of lightly salted water to the boil. Add the spaghetti and 1 tbsp of the olive oil and cook until tender, but still firm to the bite. Drain and return to the pan with the remaining olive oil. Cover, set aside and keep warm.

2 Pour the cream into a small saucepan and bring to simmering point, but do not let it boil. Pour the whisky or brandy into another small saucepan and bring to simmering point, but do not allow it to boil. Remove both pans from the heat and mix together the cream and whisky or brandy.

3 Cut the smoked salmon into thin strips and add to the cream mixture. Season with cayenne and black pepper. Just before serving, stir in the fresh coriander (cilantro) or parsley.

4 Transfer the spaghetti to a warm serving dish, pour over the sauce and toss thoroughly with 2 large forks. Scatter over the crumbled feta cheese, garnish with the coriander (cilantro) or parsley leaves and serve immediately.

COOK'S TIP

Serve this rich and luxurious dish with a green salad tossed in a lemony dressing.

Trout with Pasta Colle Acciughe & Smoked Bacon

Serves 4

INGREDIENTS

4 x 275 g/9^{1}/$_{2}$ oz trout, gutted
    and cleaned
12 anchovies in oil, drained
    and chopped
2 apples, peeled, cored and
    sliced
4 fresh mint sprigs

juice of 1 lemon
12 slices rindless, smoked,
    fatty bacon
butter, for greasing
450 g/1 lb dried tagliatelle
1 tbsp olive oil
salt and pepper

TO GARNISH:
2 apples, cored and sliced
4 fresh mint sprigs

1 Open up the cavities of each trout and wash with warm salt water.

2 Season each cavity with salt and black pepper. Divide the anchovies, sliced apples and mint sprigs between each of the cavities. Sprinkle the lemon juice into each cavity.

3 Carefully cover the whole of each trout, except the head and tail, with three slices of smoked bacon in a spiral.

4 Arrange the trout on a deep, greased baking (cookie) sheet with the loose ends of bacon tucked underneath. Season with black pepper and bake in a preheated oven at 200°C/400°F/Gas 6 for about 20 minutes, turning the trout over after 10 minutes.

5 Bring a large pan of salted water to the boil. Add the tagliatelle and oil and cook for about 12 minutes, until tender but still firm to the bite. Drain and transfer to a warm serving dish.

6 Remove the trout from the oven and arrange on the tagliatelle. Garnish with sliced apples and fresh mint sprigs and serve immediately.

Farfalle with a Medley of Seafood

Serves 4

INGREDIENTS

12 raw tiger prawns (shrimp)
12 raw shrimp
125 g/4^1/2 oz freshwater
    prawns (shrimp)
450 g/1 lb fillet of sea bream
60 g/2 oz/4 tbsp butter
12 scallops, shelled
juice and finely grated rind of
    1 lemon

pinch of saffron powder or
    threads
1 litre/1^3/4 pints/4 cups
    vegetable stock
150 ml/^{1}/4 pint/^{5}/8 cup rose
    petal vinegar (see page 98)
450 g/1 lb dried farfalle
1 tbsp olive oil

150 ml/^{1}/4 pint/^{5}/8 cup white
    wine
1 tbsp pink peppercorns
115 g/4 oz baby carrots
150 ml/^{1}/4 pint/^{5}/8 cup double
    (heavy) cream or fromage
    frais
salt and pepper
fresh parsley, to garnish

1 Peel and devein the prawns (shrimp) and shrimp. Thinly slice the sea bream. Melt the butter in a pan, add the sea bream, scallops, prawns (shrimp) and shrimp and cook for 1–2 minutes.

2 Season with black pepper. Add the lemon juice and rind. Carefully add the saffron to the cooking juices (not to the seafood).

3 Remove the seafood from the pan, set aside and keep warm.

4 Return the pan to the heat and add the vegetable stock. Bring to the boil and reduce by one third. Add the rose petal vinegar and cook for 4 minutes, until reduced.

5 Bring a pan of salted water to the boil. Add the farfalle and olive oil and

cook until tender, but still firm to the bite. Drain and transfer to a serving plate, topped with the seafood.

6 Add the wine, peppercorns, and carrots to the pan and reduce the sauce for 6 minutes. Add the cream or fromage frais and simmer for 2 minutes. Pour the sauce over the seafood and pasta, garnish and serve.

Seafood Lasagne

Serves 4

INGREDIENTS

450 g/1 lb finnan haddock,
  filleted, skin removed and
  flesh flaked
115 g/ 4 oz prawns (shrimp)
115 g/4 oz sole fillet, skin
  removed and flesh sliced
juice of 1 lemon

60 g/2 oz/4 tbsp butter
3 leeks, very thinly sliced
60 g/2 oz/$\frac{1}{2}$ cup plain
  (all purpose) flour
about 600 ml/1 pint/2$\frac{1}{3}$ cups
  milk
2 tbsp clear honey

200g/7 oz /1$\frac{3}{4}$ cups grated
  mozzarella cheese
450g/1 lb pre-cooked lasagne
60 g/2 oz/$\frac{2}{3}$ cup freshly
  grated Parmesan cheese
black pepper

1 Put the haddock fillet, prawns (shrimp) and sole fillet into a large bowl and season with black pepper and lemon juice. Set aside while you start to make the sauce.

2 Melt the butter in a large saucepan. Add the leeks and cook, stirring occasionally, for 8 minutes. Add the flour and cook, stirring constantly, for 1 minute. Gradually stir in enough milk to make a thick, creamy sauce.

3 Blend in the honey and mozzarella cheese and cook for a further 3 minutes. Remove from the heat and mix in the fish and prawns (shrimp).

4 Make alternate layers of fish sauce and lasagne in an ovenproof dish, finishing with a layer of fish sauce. Sprinkle over the grated Parmesan cheese and bake in a preheated oven at 180°C/350°F/Gas 4 for 30 minutes. Serve immediately.

VARIATION

For a cider sauce, substitute 1 finely chopped shallot for the leeks, 300 ml/ ½ pint/1¼ cups cider and 300 ml/½ pint/1¼ cups double (heavy) cream for the milk and 1 tsp mustard for the honey.

For a Tuscan sauce, substitute 1 finely chopped fennel bulb for the leeks and omit the honey.

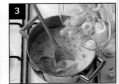

Spaghetti with Seafood Sauce

Serves 4

INGREDIENTS

225 g/8 oz dried spaghetti, broken into 15 cm/6 inch lengths
2 tbsp olive oil
300 ml/^{1}/$_2$ pint/1^1/$_4$ cups chicken stock
1 tsp lemon juice
1 small cauliflower, cut into florets (flowerets)
2 carrots, thinly sliced

115 g/4 oz mangetouts (snow peas)
60 g/2 oz/4 tbsp butter
1 onion, sliced
225 g/8 oz courgettes (zucchini), sliced
1 garlic clove, chopped
350 g/12 oz frozen, cooked, peeled prawns (shrimp), defrosted

2 tbsp chopped fresh parsley
25 g/1 oz/^{1}/$_3$ cup freshly grated Parmesan cheese
^{1}/$_2$ tsp paprika
salt and pepper
4 unpeeled, cooked prawns (shrimp), to garnish

1 Bring a pan of lightly salted water to the boil. Add the spaghetti and 1 tbsp of the olive oil and cook until tender, but still firm to the bite. Drain, toss with the remaining olive oil, cover and keep warm.

2 Bring the chicken stock and lemon juice to the boil. Add the cauliflower and carrots and cook for 3–4 minutes.

Remove from the pan and set aside. Cook the mangetouts (snow peas) for 1–2 minutes then set aside with the other vegetables.

3 Melt half the butter in a frying pan (skillet) and fry the onion and courgettes (zucchini) for 3 minutes. Add the garlic and prawns (shrimp) and cook for a further 2–3 minutes. Stir in the

reserved vegetables and heat through. Season to taste and stir in the remaining butter.

4 Transfer the spaghetti to a warm serving dish. Mix in the sauce and the chopped parsley until coated. Sprinkle over the Parmesan cheese and paprika, garnish with the unpeeled prawns (shrimp) and serve immediately.

Macaroni & Prawn (Shrimp) Bake

Serves 4

INGREDIENTS

350 g/12 oz/3 cups dried
short-cut macaroni
1 tbsp olive oil, plus extra
for brushing
90 g/3 oz/6 tbsp butter, plus
extra for greasing
2 small fennel bulbs, thinly
sliced and fronds reserved

175 g/6 oz mushrooms, thinly
sliced
175 g/6 oz peeled, cooked
prawns (shrimp)
pinch of cayenne pepper
300 ml/$^1/_2$ pint/1$^1/_4$ cups
Béchamel Sauce (see
Cook's Tip, below)

60 g/2 oz/$^2/_3$ cup freshly
grated Parmesan cheese
2 large tomatoes, sliced
1 tsp dried oregano
salt and pepper

1 Bring a pan of salted water to the boil. Add the pasta and oil and cook until tender, but still firm to the bite. Drain, return to the pan and toss in 25 g/1 oz/2 tbsp of the butter. Cover and keep warm.

2 Fry the fennel in the remaining butter for 3–4 minutes. Stir in the mushrooms and fry for 2 minutes. Stir in the prawns (shrimp), then remove the pan from the heat.

3 Stir the pasta, cayenne pepper and prawn (shrimp) mixture into the Béchamel sauce. Pour into a greased ovenproof dish. Sprinkle over the Parmesan cheese and arrange the tomato slices around the edge. Brush the tomatoes with olive oil and sprinkle over the oregano.

4 Bake in a preheated oven at 180°C/350°F/ Gas 4 for 25 minutes, until golden brown. Serve.

COOK'S TIP

For Béchamel sauce, melt 25 g/1 oz/2 tbsp butter. Stir in 25 g/1 oz/¼ cup flour and cook for 2 minutes. Gradually, stir in 300 ml/ ½ pint/1¼ cups warm milk. Add 2 tbsp finely chopped onion, 5 white peppercorns and 2 parsley sprigs. Season with salt, dried thyme and grated nutmeg. Simmer, stirring, for 15 minutes. Strain.

Pasta Parcels

Serves 4

INGREDIENTS

450 g/1 lb dried fettuccine	750 g/1 lb 10 oz large raw	125 ml/4 fl oz/^{1}/2 cup dry
150 ml/^{1}/4 pint/^{5}/8 cup Pesto	prawns (shrimp), peeled	white wine
Sauce (see page 12)	and deveined	salt and pepper
4 tsp extra virgin olive oil	2 garlic cloves, crushed	lemon wedges, to serve

1 Cut out 4 × 30 cm/ 12 inch squares of greaseproof (baking) paper.

2 Bring a large saucepan of lightly salted water to the boil. Add the fettuccine and cook for 2–3 minutes, until just softened. Drain and set aside.

3 Mix together the fettuccine and half of the Pesto Sauce. Spread out the paper squares and put 1 tsp olive oil in the middle of each. Divide the fettuccine between the squares, then divide the prawns (shrimp) and place on top of the fettuccine.

4 Mix together the remaining Pesto Sauce and the garlic and spoon it over the prawns (shrimp). Season each parcel with salt and black pepper and sprinkle with the white wine.

5 Dampen the edges of the greaseproof (baking) paper and wrap the parcels loosely, twisting the edges to seal.

6 Place the parcels on a baking (cookie) sheet and bake in a preheated oven at 200°C/400°F/ Gas 6 for 10–15 minutes. Transfer the parcels to 4 individual serving plates and serve immediately.

COOK'S TIP

Traditionally, these parcels are designed to look like money bags. The resemblance is more effective with greaseproof (baking) paper than with foil.

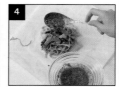

Farfallini Buttered Lobster

Serves 4

INGREDIENTS

2 x 700 g/1 lb 9 oz lobsters,
  split into halves
juice and grated rind of
  1 lemon
115 g/4 oz/^{1}/2 cup butter
4 tbsp fresh white
  breadcrumbs

2 tbsp brandy
5 tbsp double (heavy) cream
  or crème fraîche
450 g/ 1 lb dried farfallini
1 tbsp olive oil
60 g/2 oz/^{2}/3 cup freshly
  grated Parmesan cheese

salt and pepper

TO GARNISH:
1 kiwi fruit, sliced
4 unpeeled, cooked king
  prawns (shrimp)
fresh dill sprigs

1 Carefully discard the stomach sac, vein and gills from each lobster. Remove all the meat from the tail and chop. Crack the claws and legs, remove the meat and chop. Transfer the meat to a bowl and add the lemon juice and rind.

2 Clean the shells thoroughly and place in a warm oven at 170°C/325°/Gas 3 to dry out.

3 Melt 25 g/1 oz/2 tbsp of the butter in a frying pan (skillet). Add the breadcrumbs and fry for about 3 minutes, until crisp and golden brown.

4 Melt the remaining butter in a saucepan and gently cook the lobster meat. Add the brandy and cook for a further 3 minutes, then add the cream or crème fraîche and season to taste.

5 Bring a large pan of lightly salted water to the boil. Add the farfallini and olive oil and cook for about 12 minutes, until tender but still firm to the bite. Drain and spoon the pasta into the clean lobster shells. Top with the buttered lobster and sprinkle with the grated Parmesan cheese and the breadcrumbs. Grill (broil) for 2–3 minutes, until golden brown.

6 Transfer the lobster shells to a warm serving dish, garnish and serve immediately.

Pasta Shells with Mussels

Serves 4–6

INGREDIENTS

1.25 kg/2³/₄ lb mussels
225 ml/8 fl oz/1 cup dry white wine
2 large onions, chopped
115 g/4 oz/¹/₂ cup unsalted butter

6 large garlic cloves, finely chopped
5 tbsp chopped fresh parsley
300 ml/¹/₂ pint/1¹/₄ cups double (heavy) cream
400 g/14 oz dried pasta shells

1 tbsp olive oil
salt and pepper
crusty bread, to serve

1 Scrub and debeard the mussels under cold running water. Discard any that do not close immediately when tapped. Put the mussels in a pan with the wine and half of the onions. Cover and cook over a medium heat, shaking the pan frequently, until the shells open.

2 Remove from the heat. Drain the mussels and reserve the cooking liquid. Discard any mussels that have not opened. Strain the cooking liquid and reserve.

3 Fry the remaining onion in the butter for 2–3 minutes. Stir in the garlic and cook for 1 minute. Gradually stir in the reserved cooking liquid, parsley and cream. Season and leave to simmer.

4 Cook the pasta with the oil in a pan of salted water until just tender, but still firm to the bite. Drain, return to the pan, cover and keep warm.

5 Reserve a few mussels for the garnish and remove the remainder from their shells. Stir the shelled mussels into the cream sauce and warm briefly. Transfer the pasta to a serving dish. Pour over the sauce and toss well to coat. Garnish with the reserved mussels and serve with warm, crusty bread.

COOK'S TIP

Pasta shells are ideal because the sauce collects in the cavities and impregnates the pasta with flavour.

Saffron Mussel Tagliatelle

Serves 4

INGREDIENTS

1 kg/2¹/₄ lb mussels
150 ml/¹/₄ pint/⁵/₈ cup white
   wine
1 medium onion, finely
   chopped
25 g/1 oz/2 tbsp butter
2 garlic cloves, crushed

2 tsp cornflour (cornstarch)
300 ml/¹/₂ pint/1¹/₄ cups
   double (heavy) cream
pinch of saffron threads or
   saffron powder
1 egg yolk
juice of ¹/₂ lemon

450 g/1 lb dried tagliatelle
1 tbsp olive oil
salt and pepper
3 tbsp chopped fresh parsley,
   to garnish

1 Scrub and debeard the mussels under cold running water. Discard any that do not close when sharply tapped. Put the mussels in a pan with the wine and onion. Cover and cook over a high heat until the shells open.

2 Drain and reserve the cooking liquid. Discard any mussels that are still closed. Reserve a few mussels for the garnish and remove the remainder from their shells.

3 Strain the cooking liquid into a saucepan. Bring to the boil and reduce by about a half. Remove from the heat.

4 Melt the butter in a saucepan and fry the garlic for 2 minutes, until golden brown. Stir in the cornflour (cornstarch) and cook, stirring, for 1 minute. Gradually stir in the cooking liquid and the cream. Crush the saffron threads and add to the pan. Season to taste and simmer

over a low heat for 2–3 minutes, until thickened.

5 Stir in the egg yolk, lemon juice and shelled mussels. Do not allow the mixture to boil.

6 Bring a pan of salted water to the boil. Add the pasta and oil and cook until tender. Drain and transfer to a serving dish. Add the mussel sauce and toss. Garnish with the parsley and reserved mussels and serve.

Baked Scallops with Pasta in Shells

Serves 4

INGREDIENTS

12 scallops	150 ml/¼ pint/⅝ cup fish	225 g/8 oz/2 cups grated
3 tbsp olive oil	stock	Cheddar cheese
350 g/12 oz/3 cups small,	1 onion, chopped	salt and pepper
dried wholemeal (whole-	juice of 2 lemons	lime wedges, to garnish
wheat) pasta shells	150 ml/¼ pint/⅝ cup double	crusty brown bread, to serve
	(heavy) cream	

1 Remove the scallops from their shells. Scrape off the skirt and the black intestinal thread. Reserve the white part (the flesh) and the orange part (the coral or roe). Carefully ease the flesh and coral from the shell with a short, but very strong knife.

2 Wash the shells thoroughly and dry them well. Put the shells on a baking (cookie) sheet, sprinkle lightly with about two thirds of the olive oil and set aside.

3 Meanwhile, bring a large saucepan of lightly salted water to the boil. Add the pasta shells and remaining olive oil and cook for about 12 minutes, until tender, but still firm to the bite. Drain and spoon about 25 g/1 oz of pasta into each scallop shell.

4 Put the scallops, fish stock and onion in an ovenproof dish and season to taste with pepper. Cover with foil and bake in a preheated oven at 180°C/350°F/Gas 4 for 8 minutes.

5 Remove the dish from the oven. Remove the foil and, using a slotted spoon, transfer the scallops to the shells. Add 1 tbsp of the cooking liquid to each shell, drizzle with lemon juice and a little cream, and top with grated cheese.

6 Increase the oven temperature to 230°C/450°F/Gas 8 and return the scallops to the oven for 4 minutes. Serve the scallops in their shells with crusty brown bread and butter.

Vermicelli with Clams

Serves 4

INGREDIENTS

400 g/14 oz dried vermicelli, spaghetti or other long pasta
2 tbsp olive oil
25 g/1 oz/2 tbsp butter
2 onions, chopped
2 garlic cloves, chopped

2 x 200 g/7 oz jars clams in brine
125 ml/4 fl oz/¹/₂ cup white wine
4 tbsp chopped fresh parsley
¹/₂ tsp dried oregano
pinch of freshly grated nutmeg

salt and pepper

TO GARNISH:
fresh basil sprigs

1 Bring a large pan of lightly salted water to the boil. Add the pasta and half the olive oil and cook until tender, but still firm to the bite. Drain, return to the pan and add the butter. Cover the pan, shake well and keep warm.

2 Heat the remaining oil in a saucepan over a medium heat. Add the onions and fry until they are translucent. Stir in the garlic and cook for 1 minute.

3 Strain the liquid from 1 jar of clams and add the liquid to the pan, together with the wine. Stir, bring to simmering point and simmer for 3 minutes. Drain the second jar of clams and discard the liquid.

4 Add the clams, parsley and oregano to the saucepan and season with pepper and nutmeg. Lower the heat and cook until the sauce is completely heated through.

5 Transfer the pasta to a serving dish and pour over the sauce. Garnish with the basil and serve.

COOK'S TIP

There are many different types of clams found along almost every coast in the world. Those traditionally used in this dish are the tiny ones – only 2.5–5 cm/ 1–2 inches across – known in Italy as vongole.

Squid & Macaroni Stew

Serves 4–6

INGREDIENTS

225 g/8 oz/2 cups dried short-
    cut macaroni or other
    small pasta shapes
7 tbsp olive oil
2 onions, sliced

350 g/12 oz prepared squid,
    cut in 4 cm/1 1/2 inch
    strips
225 ml/8 fl oz/1 cup fish stock
150 ml/1/4 pint/5/8 cup red
    wine
2 tbsp tomato purée (paste)

350 g/12 oz tomatoes, skinned
    and thinly sliced
1 tsp dried oregano
2 bay leaves
2 tbsp chopped fresh parsley
salt and pepper
crusty bread, to serve

1 Bring a large pan of salted water to the boil. Add the pasta and 1 tbsp of oil and cook for 3 minutes. Drain and keep warm.

2 Heat the remaining oil in a pan and fry the onions until translucent. Add the squid and stock and simmer for 5 minutes. Pour in the wine and add the tomato purée (paste), tomatoes, oregano and bay leaves. Bring the sauce to the boil, season to taste and cook for 5 minutes.

3 Stir the pasta into the pan, cover and simmer for 10 minutes, or until the squid and macaroni are tender and the sauce has thickened. If the sauce remains too liquid, uncover the pan and continue cooking for a few minutes.

4 Discard the bay leaves. Reserve a little parsley and stir the remainder into the pan. Transfer to a warm serving dish and sprinkle over the remaining parsley. Serve with crusty bread.

COOK'S TIP

To prepare squid, peel off the outer skin, then cut off the head and tentacles. Extract the transparent flat oval bone from the body and discard. Remove the sac of black ink, then turn the body sac inside out. Wash in cold water. Cut off the tentacles and discard the rest; wash thoroughly.

Vegetables & Salads

The pasta recipes in this chapter offer something special for every occasion: filling vegetarian suppers, unusual vegetable side dishes, main course and side salads. You could even take many of the salads on a picnic and, of course, they are perfect as accompaniments for summer barbecues. Some are classic dishes, such as Fettuccine all'Alfredo, Spaghetti Olio e Aglio, Paglia e Fieno and Pasta & Herring Salad. Others are imaginative and sometimes surprising new combinations of vegetables and pasta. Try Mediterranean Spaghetti, Spinach & Wild Mushroom Lasagne, Ravioli with Vegetable Stuffing and Rare Beef Pasta Salad for a family meal, while Linguine with Braised Fennel, Goat's Cheese with Penne & Walnut Salad and Pasta & Garlic Mayo Salad make superb side dishes to get the tastebuds tingling.

Fettuccine all'Alfredo

Serves 4

INGREDIENTS

25 g/1 oz/2 tbsp butter
200 ml/7 fl oz/⁷⁄₈ cup double
   (heavy) cream
460 g/1 lb fresh fettuccine

1 tbsp olive oil
90 g/3 oz/1 cup freshly grated
   Parmesan cheese, plus
   extra to serve

pinch of freshly grated
   nutmeg
salt and pepper
fresh parsley sprigs, to garnish

1 Put the butter and 150 ml/¼ pint/⅝ cup of the cream in a large saucepan and bring the mixture to the boil over a medium heat. Reduce the heat and then simmer gently for about 1½ minutes, or until slightly thickened.

2 Meanwhile, bring a large pan of lightly salted water to the boil. Add the fettuccine and olive oil and cook for 2–3 minutes, until tender but still firm to the bite. Drain the fettuccine, then pour over the cream sauce.

3 Using 2 forks, toss the fettuccine in the sauce over a low heat until thoroughly coated.

4 Add the remaining cream, the Parmesan cheese and nutmeg to the fettuccine mixture and season to taste. Toss thoroughly to coat while gently heating through.

5 Transfer the fettuccine mixture to a warm serving plate and garnish with the fresh parsley sprigs. Serve immediately, handing extra grated Parmesan cheese separately.

VARIATION

This classic Roman dish is often served with the addition of strips of ham and fresh peas. Add 225 g/ 8 oz/2 cups shelled cooked peas and 175 g/6 oz ham strips with the Parmesan cheese in step 4.

184

Macaroni Bake

Serves 4

INGREDIENTS

460 g/1 lb/4 cups dried short-cut macaroni
1 tbsp olive oil
60 g/2 oz/4 tbsp beef dripping

460 g/1 lb potatoes, thinly sliced
460 g/1 lb onions, sliced
225 g/8 oz/2 cups grated mozzarella cheese

150 ml/5 fl oz/⁵⁄₈ cup double (heavy) cream
salt and pepper
crusty brown bread and butter, to serve

1 Bring a large saucepan of lightly salted water to the boil. Add the macaroni and olive oil and cook for about 12 minutes, until tender but still firm to the bite. Drain the macaroni thoroughly and set aside.

2 Melt the dripping in a large flameproof casserole, then remove from the heat.

3 Make alternate layers of potatoes, onions, macaroni and grated cheese in the dish, seasoning well with salt and pepper between each layer and finishing with a layer of cheese on top. Finally, pour the cream over the top layer of cheese.

4 Bake in a preheated oven at 200°C/400°F/ Gas 6 for 25 minutes. Remove the dish from the oven and carefully brown the top of the bake under a hot grill (broiler).

5 Serve the bake straight from the dish with crusty brown bread and butter as a main course.

Alternatively, serve as a vegetable accompaniment with your favourite main course.

VARIATION

For a stronger flavour, use mozzarella affumicata, *a smoked version of this cheese, or* Gruyère *(Swiss) cheese instead of the mozzarella.*

Creamy Pasta & Broccoli

Serves 4

INGREDIENTS

60 g/2 oz/4 tbsp butter
1 large onion, finely chopped
450 g/1 lb dried ribbon pasta
460 g/1 lb broccoli, broken
   into florets (flowerets)

150 ml/$^1\!/_4$ pint/$^5\!/_8$ cup
   boiling vegetable stock
1 tbsp plain (all purpose) flour
150 ml/$^1\!/_4$ pint/$^5\!/_8$ cup single
   (light) cream

60 g/2 oz/$^1\!/_2$ cup grated
   mozzarella cheese
freshly grated nutmeg
salt and white pepper
fresh apple slices, to garnish

1 Melt half of the butter in a large saucepan over a medium heat. Add the onion and fry for 4 minutes.

2 Add the pasta and broccoli to the pan and cook, stirring constantly, for 2 minutes. Add the vegetable stock, bring back to the boil and simmer for a further 12 minutes. Season well with salt and white pepper.

3 Meanwhile, melt the remaining butter in a saucepan over a medium heat. Stir in the flour and cook for 2 minutes. Gradually stir in the cream and bring to simmering point, but do not boil. Add the grated cheese and season with salt and a little freshly grated nutmeg.

4 Drain the pasta and broccoli mixture and pour over the cheese sauce. Cook, stirring occasionally, for about 2 minutes. Transfer the pasta and broccoli mixture to a warm, large, deep serving dish and serve garnished with slices of fresh apple.

VARIATION

This dish would also be delicious and look just as colourful made with Cape broccoli, which is actually a purple variety of cauliflower and not broccoli at all.

Paglia e Fieno

Serves 4

INGREDIENTS

60 g/2 oz/4 tbsp butter
900 g/1 lb fresh peas, shelled
200 ml/7 fl oz/ ⁷/₈ cup double
(heavy) cream
460 g/1 lb mixed fresh green
and white spaghetti or
tagliatelle

1 tbsp olive oil
60 g/2 oz/ ²/₃ cup freshly
grated Parmesan cheese,
plus extra to serve

pinch of freshly grated
nutmeg
salt and pepper

1 Melt the butter in a large saucepan. Add the peas and cook, over a low heat, for 2–3 minutes.

2 Using a measuring jug (pitcher), pour 150 ml/ 5 fl oz/⅝ cup of the cream into the pan, bring to the boil and simmer for 1–1½ minutes, until slightly thickened. Remove the pan from the heat.

3 Meanwhile, bring a large pan of lightly salted water to the boil.

Add the spaghetti or tagliatelle and olive oil and cook for 2–3 minutes, until just tender but still firm to the bite. Remove the pan from the heat, drain the pasta thoroughly and return to the pan.

4 Add the peas and cream sauce to the pasta. Return the pan to the heat and add the remaining cream and the Parmesan cheese and season to taste with salt, black pepper and grated nutmeg.

5 Using 2 forks, gently toss the pasta to coat with the peas and cream sauce, while heating through.

6 Transfer the pasta to a serving dish and serve immediately, with extra Parmesan cheese.

Green Tagliatelle with Garlic

Serves 4

INGREDIENTS

2 tbsp walnut oil
1 bunch spring onions
    (scallions), sliced
2 garlic cloves, thinly sliced
250 g/8 oz/3¹/4 cups sliced
    mushrooms
450 g/1 lb fresh green and
    white tagliatelle

1 tbsp olive oil
225 g/8 oz frozen spinach,
    thawed and drained
115 g/4 oz/¹/2 cup full-fat soft
    cheese with garlic and
    herbs
4 tbsp single (light) cream

60 g/2 oz/¹/2 cup chopped,
    unsalted pistachio nuts
2 tbsp shredded fresh basil
salt and pepper
fresh basil sprigs, to garnish
Italian bread, to serve

1 Heat the walnut oil in a large frying pan (skillet). Add the spring onions (scallions) and garlic and fry for 1 minute, until just softened.

2 Add the mushrooms to the pan, stir well, cover and cook over a low heat for about 5 minutes, until softened.

3 Meanwhile, bring a large saucepan of lightly salted water to the boil. Add the tagliatelle and olive oil and cook for 3–5 minutes, until tender but still firm to the bite. Drain and return to the saucepan.

4 Add the spinach to the frying pan (skillet) and heat through for 1–2 minutes. Add the cheese to the pan and allow to melt slightly. Stir in the cream and continue to cook, without allowing the mixture to come to the boil, until warmed through.

5 Pour the sauce over the tagliatelle, season with salt and black pepper to taste and mix well. Heat through gently, stirring constantly, for 2–3 minutes.

6 Transfer the pasta to a serving dish and sprinkle with the pistachio nuts and shredded basil. Garnish with the basil sprigs and serve with the Italian bread of your choice.

Spaghetti Olio e Aglio

Serves 4

INGREDIENTS

125 ml/4 fl oz/$^{1}/_{2}$ cup olive oil
3 garlic cloves, crushed
460 g/1 lb fresh spaghetti

3 tbsp roughly chopped fresh
parsley

salt and pepper

1 Reserve 1 tbsp of the olive oil and heat the remainder in a medium saucepan. Add the garlic and a pinch of salt and cook over a low heat, stirring constantly, until golden brown, then remove the pan from the heat. Do not allow the garlic to burn as it will taint its flavour. (If it does burn, you will have to start all over again!)

2 Meanwhile, bring a large saucepan of lightly salted water to the boil. Add the spaghetti and remaining olive oil and cook for 2–3 minutes, until tender, but still firm to the bite. Drain the spaghetti thoroughly and return to the pan.

3 Add the oil and garlic mixture to the spaghetti and toss to coat thoroughly. Season with pepper, add the chopped fresh parsley and toss to coat again.

4 Transfer the spaghetti to a warm serving dish and serve immediately.

COOK'S TIP

It is worth buying the best-quality olive oil for dishes such as this one which makes a feature of its flavour. Extra virgin oil is produced from the first pressing and has the lowest acidity. It is more expensive than other types of olive oil, but has the finest flavour. Virgin olive oil is slightly more acid, but is also well flavoured. Oil simply labelled pure has usually been heat-treated and refined by mechanical means and, consequently, lacks character and flavour.

Patriotic Pasta

Serves 4

INGREDIENTS

460 g/1 lb/4 cups dried farfalle	460 g/1 lb cherry tomatoes	salt and pepper
4 tbsp olive oil	90 g/3 oz rocket (arugula)	Pecorino cheese, to garnish

1 Bring a large saucepan of lightly salted water to the boil. Add the farfalle and 1 tbsp of the olive oil and cook until tender, but still firm to the bite. Drain the farfalle thoroughly and return to the pan.

2 Cut the cherry tomatoes in half and trim the rocket (arugula).

3 Heat the remaining olive oil in a large saucepan. Add the tomatoes and cook for 1 minute. Add the farfalle and the rocket (arugula) and stir gently to mix. Heat through and season to taste with salt and black pepper.

4 Meanwhile, using a vegetable peeler, shave thin slices of Pecorino cheese.

5 Transfer the farfalle and vegetables to a warm serving dish. Garnish with the Pecorino cheese shavings and serve immediately.

COOK'S TIP

Pecorino cheese is a hard sheep's milk cheese which resembles Parmesan and is often used for grating over a variety of dishes. It has a sharp flavour and is only used in small quantities.

COOK'S TIP

Rocket (arugula) is a small plant with irregular-shaped leaves rather like those of turnip tops (greens). The flavour is distinctively peppery and slightly reminiscent of radish. It has always been popular in Italy, both in salads and for serving with pasta and has recently enjoyed a revival in Britain and the United States, where it has now become very fashionable.

Mediterranean Spaghetti

Serves 4

INGREDIENTS

2 tbsp olive oil
1 large, red onion, chopped
2 garlic cloves, crushed
1 tbsp lemon juice
4 baby aubergines (eggplants),
    quartered

600 ml/1 pint/2¹/₂ cups
    passata (sieved tomatoes)
2 tsp caster (superfine) sugar
2 tbsp tomato purée (paste)
400 g/14 oz can artichoke
    hearts, drained and halved

115 g/4 oz/1 cup stoned
    (pitted) black olives
350 g/12 oz dried spaghetti
25 g/1 oz/2 tbsp butter
salt and pepper
fresh basil sprigs, to garnish
olive bread, to serve

1 Heat 1 tbsp of the olive oil in a large frying pan (skillet). Add the onion, garlic, lemon juice and aubergines (eggplants) and cook over a low heat for 4–5 minutes, until the onion and aubergines (eggplants) are lightly golden brown.

2 Pour in the passata (sieved tomatoes), season to taste with salt and black pepper and stir in the caster (superfine) sugar and tomato purée (paste). Bring to the boil, then simmer, stirring occasionally, for 20 minutes.

3 Gently stir in the artichoke hearts and black olives and cook for 5 minutes.

4 Meanwhile, bring a large saucepan of lightly salted water to the boil. Add the spaghetti and the remaining oil and cook for 7–8 minutes, until tender but still firm to the bite.

5 Drain the spaghetti thoroughly and toss with the butter. Transfer the spaghetti to a large serving dish.

6 Pour the vegetable sauce over the spaghetti, garnish with the sprigs of fresh basil and serve immediately with olive bread.

Spinach & Wild Mushroom Lasagne

Serves 4

INGREDIENTS

115 g/4 oz/8 tbsp butter, plus
    extra for greasing
2 garlic cloves, finely chopped
115 g/4 oz shallots
225 g/8 oz wild mushrooms,
    such as chanterelles
450 g/1 lb spinach, cooked,
    drained and finely chopped

225 g/8 oz/2 cups grated
    Cheddar cheese
$^1/_4$ tsp freshly grated nutmeg
1 tsp chopped fresh basil
60 g/2 oz plain (all purpose)
    flour
600 ml/1 pint/$2^1/_2$ cups hot
    milk

60 g/2 oz/ $^2/_3$ cup grated
    Cheshire cheese
salt and pepper
8 sheets pre-cooked lasagne
watercress salad, to serve

1 Lightly grease an ovenproof dish.

2 Melt 60 g/2 oz/4 tbsp of the butter in a saucepan. Add the garlic, shallots and wild mushrooms and fry over a low heat for 3 minutes. Stir in the spinach, Cheddar cheese, nutmeg and basil. Season well and set aside.

3 Melt the remaining butter in another saucepan over a low heat.

Stir in the flour and cook for 1 minute. Gradually stir in the hot milk, whisking constantly until smooth. Stir in 25 g/1 oz/¼ cup of the Cheshire cheese and season to taste.

4 Spread half of the mushroom and spinach mixture over the base of the prepared dish. Cover with a layer of lasagne and then with half of the cheese sauce. Repeat and then sprinkle over the

remaining cheese. Bake in a preheated oven at 200°C/ 400°F/Gas 6 for 30 minutes, until golden brown. Serve hot.

VARIATION

Substitute 4 (bell) peppers for the spinach. Roast in a preheated oven at 200°C/ 400°F/Gas 6 for 20 minutes. Rub off the skins under cold water, deseed and chop before using.

Ravioli with Vegetable Stuffing

Serves 4

INGREDIENTS

450 g/1 lb Basic Pasta Dough (see page 4)	STUFFING:	120 ml/4 fl oz/^{1}/$_2$ cup olive oil
1 tbsp olive oil	2 large aubergines (eggplants)	60 g/2 oz tomato purée
90 g/3 oz/6 tbsp butter	3 large courgettes (zucchini)	(paste)
150 ml/5 fl oz/^{5}/$_8$ cup single (light) cream	6 large tomatoes	^{1}/$_2$ tsp chopped fresh basil
	1 large green (bell) pepper	salt and pepper
75 g/3 oz/1 cup freshly grated Parmesan cheese	1 large red (bell) pepper	fresh basil sprig, to garnish
	3 garlic cloves	
	1 large onion	

1 To make the stuffing, cut the aubergines (eggplants) and courgettes (zucchini) into 2.5 cm/ 1 inch chunks. Sprinkle the aubergine (eggplant) with salt and set aside for 20 minutes. Rinse and drain.

2 Blanch the tomatoes in boiling water for 2 minutes. Drain, skin and chop the flesh. Core and seed the (bell) peppers and cut into 2.5 cm/1 inch dice. Chop the garlic and onion.

3 Heat the oil in a saucepan and fry the garlic and onion for 3 minutes. Stir in the remaining stuffing ingredients and season with salt and pepper. Cover and simmer for 20 minutes, stirring frequently.

4 Roll out the pasta dough and cut out 7.5 cm/3 inch rounds. Put a spoonful of the vegetable stuffing on each round. Dampen the edges slightly and fold the pasta rounds over, pressing to seal.

5 Bring a pan of salted water to the boil. Add the ravioli and the oil and cook for 3–4 minutes. Drain and transfer to a dish, dotting each layer with butter. Pour over the cream and sprinkle over the Parmesan cheese. Bake in a preheated oven at 200°C/400°F/Gas 6 for 20 minutes. Garnish and serve

Courgette (Zucchini) & Aubergine (Eggplant) Lasagne

Serves 6

INGREDIENTS

1 kg/2¹/₄ lb aubergines
(eggplants)
8 tbsp olive oil
25 g/1 oz/2 tbsp garlic and
herb butter
450 g/1 lb courgettes
(zucchini), sliced

225 g/8 oz/2 cups grated
mozzarella cheese
600 ml/1 pint/2¹/₂ cups
passata (sieved tomatoes)
6 sheets pre-cooked green
lasagne

600 ml/1 pint/2¹/₂ cups
Béchamel Sauce (see page
166)
60 g/2 oz/²/₃ cup freshly
grated Parmesan cheese
1 tsp dried oregano
salt and black pepper

1 Thinly slice the aubergines (eggplants), sprinkle with salt and set aside for 20 minutes. Rinse and pat dry.

2 Heat 4 tbsp of the oil in a large frying pan (skillet). Fry half the aubergine (eggplant) slices over a low heat for 6–7 minutes, until golden. Drain then repeat with the remaining oil and aubergine (eggplant) slices.

3 Melt the garlic and herb butter in the frying pan (skillet) and fry the courgettes (zucchini) for 5–6 minutes, until golden brown. Drain.

4 Place half the aubergine (eggplant) and courgette (zucchini) slices in a large ovenproof dish. Season with pepper and sprinkle over half the mozzarella cheese. Spoon over half the passata (sieved tomatoes) and top with 3 sheets of lasagne. Repeat the process, ending with a layer of lasagne.

5 Spoon over the Béchamel sauce and sprinkle over the Parmesan cheese and oregano. Put the dish on a baking (cookie) sheet and bake in a preheated oven at 220°C/425°F/Gas 7 for 30–35 minutes, until golden brown. Serve.

Pasta & Bean Casserole

Serves 6

INGREDIENTS

225 g/8 oz/1¹/₄ cups dried
  haricot (navy) beans,
  soaked overnight
  and drained
225 g/8 oz dried penne
6 tbsp olive oil
850 ml/1¹/₂ pints /3¹/₂ cups
  vegetable stock
2 large onions, sliced

2 garlic cloves, chopped
2 bay leaves
1 tsp dried oregano
1 tsp dried thyme
5 tbsp red wine
2 tbsp tomato purée (paste)
2 celery sticks (stalks), sliced
1 fennel bulb, sliced

115 g/4 oz/1⁵/₈ cups sliced
  mushrooms
250 g/8 oz tomatoes, sliced
1 tsp dark muscovado sugar
4 tbsp dry white breadcrumbs
salt and pepper
salad leaves (greens) and
  crusty bread, to serve

1 Put the haricot (navy) beans in a large saucepan and add cold water to cover. Bring to the boil and boil vigorously for 20 minutes. Drain, set aside and keep warm.

2 Bring a large saucepan of lightly salted water to the boil. Add the penne and 1 tbsp of the olive oil and cook for about 3 minutes. Drain the pasta, set aside and keep warm.

3 Put the beans in a large, flameproof casserole. Add the vegetable stock and stir in the remaining olive oil, the onions, garlic, bay leaves, oregano, thyme, wine and tomato purée (paste). Bring to the boil, then cover and cook in a preheated oven at 180°C/350°F/Gas 4 for 2 hours.

4 Add the penne, celery, fennel, mushrooms

and tomatoes to the casserole and season to taste with salt and pepper. Stir in the muscovado sugar and sprinkle over the breadcrumbs. Cover the dish and cook in the oven for 1 further hour.

5 Serve hot with salad leaves (greens) and crusty bread.

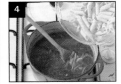

Creamed Spaghetti & Mushrooms

Serves 4

INGREDIENTS

60 g/2 oz/4 tbsp butter	150 ml/^{1}/4 pint/^{5}/8 cup double	450g /1 lb dried spaghetti
2 tbsp olive oil	(heavy) cream	1 tbsp freshly chopped parsley
6 shallots, sliced	2 tbsp port	salt and pepper
450 g/1 lb/6 cups sliced	115 g/4 oz sun-dried	6 triangles of fried white
button mushrooms	tomatoes, chopped	bread, to serve
1 tsp plain (all purpose) flour	freshly grated nutmeg	

1 Heat the butter and 1 tbsp of the oil in a large pan. Add the shallots and cook over a medium heat for 3 minutes. Add the mushrooms and cook over a low heat for 2 minutes. Season with salt and black pepper, sprinkle over the flour and cook, stirring constantly, for 1 minute.

2 Gradually stir in the cream and port, add the sun-dried tomatoes and a pinch of grated nutmeg and cook over a low heat for 8 minutes.

3 Bring a large saucepan of lightly salted water to the boil. Add the spaghetti and remaining olive oil and cook for 12–14 minutes, until tender but still firm to the bite.

4 Drain the spaghetti and return to the pan. Pour over the mushroom sauce and cook for 3 minutes. Transfer the spaghetti and mushroom sauce to a large serving plate and sprinkle over the chopped parsley. Serve with crispy triangles of fried bread.

VARIATION

Non-vegetarians could add 115 g/4 oz Parma ham (prosciutto), cut into thin strips and heated gently in 25 g/1 oz/2 tbsp butter, to the pasta along with the mushroom sauce.

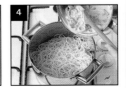

Vegetable Pasta Stir-fry

Serves 4

INGREDIENTS

400 g/14 oz dried wholemeal (whole-wheat) pasta shells or other short pasta shapes
1 tbsp olive oil
2 carrots, thinly sliced
115 g/4 oz baby corn cobs
3 tbsp corn oil
2.5 cm/1 inch piece fresh root ginger, thinly sliced
1 large onion, thinly sliced

1 garlic clove, thinly sliced
3 celery sticks (stalks), thinly sliced
1 small red (bell) pepper, cored, seeded and cut into matchstick strips
1 small green (bell) pepper, cored, seeded and cut into matchstick strips
1 tsp cornflour (cornstarch)

2 tbsp water
3 tbsp soy sauce
3 tbsp dry sherry
1 tsp clear honey
a dash of hot pepper sauce (optional)
salt
red (bell) pepper, finely sliced, to garnish

1 Bring a large pan of salted water to the boil. Add the pasta and olive oil and cook until tender, but still firm to the bite. Drain and keep warm.

2 Bring a saucepan of lightly salted water to the boil. Add the carrots and corn cobs and cook for 2 minutes. Drain, refresh in cold water and drain again.

3 Heat the corn oil in a preheated wok or large frying pan (skillet). Add the ginger and stir-fry over a medium heat for 1 minute. Remove the ginger with a slotted spoon and discard.

4 Add the onion, garlic, celery and (bell) peppers to the pan and stir-fry for 2 minutes. Add the carrots and baby corn cobs and stir-fry for a further

2 minutes. Stir in the drained pasta.

5 Mix the cornflour (cornstarch) and water to make a smooth paste. Stir in the soy sauce, sherry and honey. Pour the cornflour mixture into the pasta and cook, stirring occasionally, for 2 minutes. Stir in the pepper sauce, if liked. Transfer to a serving dish, garnish and serve.

Macaroni & Corn Pancakes

Serves 4

INGREDIENTS

2 corn cobs
60 g/2 oz/4 tbsp butter
115 g/4 oz red (bell) peppers,
   cored, seeded and finely
   diced
285 g/10 oz/2^1/2 cups dried
   short-cut macaroni

150 ml/^{1}/4 pint/^{5}/8 cup double
   (heavy) cream
25 g/1 oz/^{1}/4 cup plain (all
   purpose) flour
4 egg yolks
4 tbsp olive oil
salt and pepper

TO SERVE:
oyster mushrooms
fried leeks

1 Bring a pan of water to the boil, add the corn cobs and cook for about 8 minutes. Drain and refresh under cold running water for 3 minutes. Carefully cut away the kernels and set aside to dry.

2 Melt 25 g/1 oz/2 tbsp of the butter in a frying pan (skillet). Add the (bell) peppers and cook over a low heat for about 4 minutes. Drain and pat dry with kitchen paper (towels).

3 Bring a large saucepan of lightly salted water to the boil. Add the macaroni and cook for about 12 minutes, until tender but still firm to the bite. Drain the macaroni and leave to cool in cold water until required.

4 Beat together the cream, flour, a pinch of salt and the egg yolks in a bowl until smooth. Add the corn and (bell) peppers to the cream and egg mixture. Drain the macaroni and

then toss into the corn and cream mixture. Season well with black pepper to taste.

5 Heat the remaining butter with the oil in a large frying pan (skillet). Drop spoonfuls of the mixture into the pan and press down until the mixture forms a flat pancake. Fry until golden on both sides, and all the mixture is used up. Serve with oyster mushrooms and fried leeks.

Vermicelli Flan

Serves 4

INGREDIENTS

75 g/3 oz/6 tbsp butter, plus extra, for greasing	1 green (bell) pepper, cored, seeded and sliced into thin rings	freshly grated nutmeg
225 g/8 oz dried vermicelli or spaghetti	150 ml/^{1}/4 pint/^{5}/8 cup milk	1 tbsp freshly grated Parmesan cheese
1 tbsp olive oil	3 eggs, lightly beaten	salt and pepper
1 onion, chopped	2 tbsp double (heavy) cream	tomato and basil salad, to serve
140 g/5 oz button mushrooms	1 tsp dried oregano	

1 Generously grease a 20 cm/8 inch loose-based flan tin (pan).

2 Bring a large pan of lightly salted water to the boil. Add the vermicelli and olive oil and cook until tender, but still firm to the bite. Drain, return to the pan and toss in 25 g/1 oz/2 tbsp of the butter to coat.

3 Press the pasta on to the base and around the sides of the flan tin (pan) to make a flan case.

4 Melt the remaining butter in a frying pan (skillet) and fry the onion until it is translucent.

5 Add the mushrooms and (bell) pepper rings to the frying pan (skillet) and cook, stirring, for 2–3 minutes. Spoon the onion, mushroom and (bell) pepper mixture into the flan case and press it evenly into the base.

6 Beat together the milk, eggs and cream, stir in the oregano and season to taste with nutmeg and black pepper. Carefully pour the mixture over the vegetables and sprinkle over the cheese.

7 Bake the flan in a preheated oven at 180°C/350°F/Gas 4 for 40–45 minutes, until the filling has set.

8 Slide the flan out of the tin (pan) and serve warm with a tomato and basil salad.

Fettuccine with Olive, Garlic & Walnut Sauce

Serves 4–6

INGREDIENTS

2 thick slices wholemeal (whole-wheat) bread, crusts removed
300 ml/^{1}/2 pint/1^1/4 cups milk
275/9^1/2 oz/2^1/2 cups shelled walnuts

2 garlic cloves, crushed
115 g/4 oz/1 cup stoned (pitted) black olives
60 g/2 oz/^{2}/3 cup freshly grated Parmesan cheese
8 tbsp extra virgin olive oil

150 ml/^{1}/4 pint/^{5}/8 cup double (heavy) cream
460 g/1 lb fresh fettuccine
salt and pepper
2–3 tbsp chopped fresh parsley

---

1 Put the bread in a shallow dish, pour over the milk and set aside to soak until the liquid has been absorbed.

2 Spread the walnuts out on a baking (cookie) sheet and toast in a preheated oven at 190°C/375°F/Gas 5 for about 5 minutes, until golden. Set aside to cool.

3 Put the soaked bread, walnuts, garlic, olives, Parmesan cheese and 6 tbsp of the olive oil in a food processor and work to make a purée. Season to taste with salt and black pepper and stir in the cream.

4 Bring a large pan of lightly salted water to the boil. Add the fettuccine and 1 tbsp of the remaining oil and cook for 2–3 minutes, until tender but still firm to the bite. Drain the fettuccine thoroughly and toss with the remaining olive oil.

5 Divide the fettuccine between individual serving plates and spoon the olive, garlic and walnut sauce on top. Sprinkle over the fresh parsley and serve.

Linguine with Braised Fennel

Serves 4

INGREDIENTS

6 fennel bulbs
150 ml/¼ pint/⅝ cup
    vegetable stock
25 g/1 oz/2 tbsp butter

6 slices rindless, smoked
    bacon, diced
6 shallots, quartered
25 g/1 oz/¼ cup plain (all
    purpose) flour

7 tbsp double (heavy) cream
1 tbsp Madeira
450 g/1 lb dried linguine
1 tbsp olive oil
salt and pepper

1 Trim the fennel bulbs, then gently peel off and reserve the first layer of the bulbs. Cut the bulbs into quarters and put them in a large saucepan, together with the vegetable stock and the reserved outer layers. Bring to the boil, lower the heat and simmer for 5 minutes.

2 Using a slotted spoon, transfer the fennel to a large dish. Discard the outer layers of the fennel bulb. Bring the vegetable stock to the boil and allow to reduce by half. Set aside.

3 Melt the butter in a frying pan (skillet). Add the bacon and shallots and fry for 4 minutes. Add the flour, reduced stock, cream and Madeira and cook, stirring constantly, for 3 minutes, until the sauce is smooth. Season to taste and pour over the fennel.

4 Bring a large saucepan of lightly salted water to the boil. Add the linguine and olive oil and cook for 10 minutes, until tender but still firm to the bite. Drain and transfer to a deep ovenproof dish.

5 Add the fennel and sauce and braise in a preheated oven at 180°C/ 350°F/Gas 4 for 20 minutes. Serve immediately.

COOK'S TIP

Fennel will keep in the salad drawer of the refrigerator for 2–3 days, but it is best eaten as fresh as possible. Cut surfaces turn brown quickly, so do not prepare it too much in advance of cooking.

Baked Aubergines (Eggplant) with Pasta

Serves 4

INGREDIENTS
---

225 g/8 oz dried penne or other short pasta shapes
4 tbsp olive oil, plus extra for brushing
2 aubergines (eggplants)
1 large onion, chopped

2 garlic cloves, crushed
400 g/14 oz can chopped tomatoes
2 tsp dried oregano
60 g/2 oz mozzarella cheese, thinly sliced

25 g/1 oz/^{1}/$_3$ cup freshly grated Parmesan cheese
2 tbsp dry breadcrumbs
salt and pepper
salad leaves (greens), to serve

---

1 Bring a pan of salted water to the boil. Add the pasta and 1 tbsp of the olive oil and cook until tender. Drain, return to the pan, cover and keep warm.

2 Cut the aubergines (eggplants) in half lengthways and score around the inside, being careful not to pierce the shells. Scoop out the flesh then brush the insides of the shells with oil. Chop the flesh and set aside.

3 Fry the onion in the remaining oil until translucent. Add the garlic and fry for 1 minute. Stir in the chopped aubergine (eggplant) and fry for 5 minutes. Add the tomatoes, oregano and seasoning. Bring to the boil and simmer for 10 minutes. Remove from the heat and stir in the pasta.

4 Brush a baking (cookie) sheet with oil and arrange the aubergine

(eggplant) shells in a single layer. Divide half the tomato and pasta mixture between them. Sprinkle over the mozzarella, then pile the remaining tomato and pasta mixture on top. Mix the Parmesan cheese and breadcrumbs and sprinkle over the top.

5 Bake in a preheated oven at 200°C/400°F/Gas 6 for 25 minutes, until golden brown. Serve with salad leaves (greens).

Pasta with Green Vegetable Sauce

Serves 4

INGREDIENTS

225 g/8 oz/2 cups dried gemelli or other pasta shapes	225 g/8 oz asparagus spears	freshly grated nutmeg
1 tbsp olive oil	115 g/4 oz mangetout (snow peas)	2 tbsp chopped fresh parsley
1 head green broccoli, cut into florets (flowerets)	115 g/4 oz frozen peas	2 tbsp freshly grated Parmesan cheese
2 courgettes (zucchini), sliced	25 g/1 oz/2 tbsp butter	salt and pepper
	3 tbsp vegetable stock	
	4 tbsp double (heavy) cream	

1 Bring a large saucepan of lightly salted water to the boil. Add the pasta and olive oil and cook until tender, but still firm to the bite. Drain, return to the pan, cover and keep warm.

2 Steam the broccoli, courgettes (zucchini), asparagus spears and mangetout (snow peas) over a pan of boiling salted water until they begin to soften. Remove from the heat and refresh in cold water. Drain and set aside.

3 Bring a small pan of lightly salted water to the boil. Add the frozen peas and cook for 3 minutes. Drain the peas, refresh in cold water and then drain again. Set aside with the other vegetables.

4 Put the butter and vegetable stock in a pan over a medium heat. Add all of the vegetables, reserving a few of the asparagus spears, and toss until they have thoroughly heated through.

5 Stir in the double (heavy) cream and heat through, without bringing to the boil. Season to taste with salt, pepper and nutmeg.

6 Transfer the pasta to a warmed serving dish and stir in the chopped parsley. Spoon over the vegetable sauce and sprinkle over the Parmesan cheese. Arrange the reserved asparagus spears in a pattern on top and serve immediately.

Niçoise with Pasta Shells

Serves 4

INGREDIENTS

350 g/12 oz dried small pasta
  shells
1 tbsp olive oil
115 g/4 oz French (green)
  beans
50 g/1³/₄ oz can anchovies,
  drained
25 ml/1 fl oz/¹/₈ cup milk
2 small crisp lettuces

460 g/1 lb or 3 large beef
  tomatoes
4 hard-boiled (hard-cooked)
  eggs
225 g/8 oz can tuna, drained
115 g/4 oz/1 cup stoned
  (pitted) black olives
salt and pepper

VINAIGRETTE DRESSING:
50 ml/2 fl oz extra virgin olive
  oil
25 ml/1 fl oz white wine
  vinegar
1 tsp wholegrain mustard
salt and pepper

1 Bring a large saucepan of lightly salted water to the boil. Add the pasta and the olive oil and cook until tender, but still firm to the bite. Drain and refresh in cold water.

2 Bring a small saucepan of lightly salted water to the boil. Add the beans and cook for 10–12 minutes, until tender but still firm to the bite. Drain, refresh in cold water, drain thoroughly once more and then set aside.

3 Put the anchovies in a shallow bowl, pour over the milk and set aside for 10 minutes. Meanwhile, tear the lettuces into large pieces. Blanch the tomatoes in boiling water for 1–2 minutes, then drain, skin and roughly chop the flesh. Shell the eggs and cut into quarters. Cut the tuna into large chunks.

4 Drain the anchovies and the pasta. Put all of the salad ingredients, the beans and the olives into a large bowl and gently mix together.

5 To make the vinaigrette dressing, beat together all the ingredients and keep in the refrigerator until required. Just before serving, pour the vinaigrette dressing over the salad.

Pasta & Herring Salad

Serves 4

INGREDIENTS

250 g/9 oz dried pasta shells	2 large tart apples	6 pickled onions
5 tbsp olive oil	2 baby frisée lettuces	6 pickled gherkins (dill pickles)
400 g/14 oz rollmop herrings in brine	2 baby beetroot (beet)	2 tbsp capers
6 boiled potatoes	4 hard-boiled (hard-cooked) eggs	3 tbsp of tarragon vinegar
		salt and pepper

---

1 Bring a large saucepan of lightly salted water to the boil. Add the pasta and 1 tbsp of the olive oil and cook until tender, but still firm to the bite. Drain the pasta thoroughly and then refresh in cold water.

2 Cut the herrings, potatoes, apples, frisée lettuces and beetroot (beet) into small pieces. Put all of these ingredients into a large salad bowl.

3 Drain the pasta thoroughly and add to the salad bowl. Toss lightly to mix the pasta and herring mixture together.

4 Carefully shell and slice the eggs. Garnish the salad with the slices of egg, pickled onions gherkins (dill pickles) and capers, sprinkle with the remaining olive oil and the tarragon vinegar and serve immediately.

COOK'S TIP

Store this salad, without the dressing, in a container in the refrigerator.

COOK'S TIP

Tarragon vinegar is available from most supermarkets, but you can easily make your own. Add a bunch of fresh tarragon to a bottle of white or red wine vinegar and leave to infuse for 48 hours. It is important to ensure that the tarragon is as fresh as possible and to discard any blemished leaves.

Neapolitan Seafood Salad with Campanelle

Serves 4

INGREDIENTS

450 g/1 lb prepared squid, cut into strips	300 ml/^{1}/$_2$ pint/1^1/$_4$ cups olive oil	1 bunch fresh parsley, finely chopped
750 g/1 lb 10 oz cooked mussels	225 g/8 oz/2 cups dried campanelle or other small pasta shapes	4 large tomatoes, quartered or sliced
450 g/1 lb cooked cockles in brine	juice of 1 lemon	mixed salad leaves (greens)
150 ml/^{1}/$_2$ pint/^{5}/$_8$ cup white wine	1 bunch chives, snipped	salt and pepper
		sprigs of fresh basil, to garnish

1 Put all of the seafood into a large bowl, pour over the wine and half the olive oil, and set aside for 6 hours.

2 Put the seafood mixture into a saucepan and simmer over a low heat for 10 minutes. Set aside to cool.

3 Bring a large saucepan of lightly salted water to the boil. Add the pasta and 1 tbsp of the remaining olive oil and cook until tender, but still firm to the bite. Drain thoroughly and refresh in cold water.

4 Strain off about half of the cooking liquid from the seafood and discard the rest. Mix in the lemon juice, chives, parsley and the remaining olive oil. Season to taste with salt and pepper. Drain the pasta and add to the seafood.

5 Cut the tomatoes into quarters. Shred the salad leaves (greens) and arrange them at the base of a salad bowl. Spoon in the seafood salad and garnish with the quartered or sliced tomatoes and a sprig of basil.

Pasta Salad with Red & White Cabbage

Serves 4

INGREDIENTS

260 g/9 oz/2¹/₄ cups dried
   short-cut macaroni
5 tbsp olive oil
1 large red cabbage, shredded

1 large white cabbage,
   shredded
2 large apples, diced
260 g/9 oz cooked smoked
   bacon or ham, diced

8 tbsp wine vinegar
1 tbsp sugar
salt and pepper

1 Bring a large saucepan of lightly salted water to the boil. Add the macaroni and 1 tbsp of the olive oil and cook until tender, but still firm to the bite. Drain the pasta, then refresh in cold water. Drain again and set aside.

2 Bring a large saucepan of lightly salted water to the boil. Add the shredded red cabbage and cook for 5 minutes. Drain thoroughly and set aside to cool.

3 Bring a large saucepan of lightly salted water to the boil. Add the white cabbage and cook for 5 minutes. Drain thoroughly and set aside to cool.

4 In a large bowl, mix together the pasta, red cabbage and apple. In a separate bowl, mix together the white cabbage and bacon or ham.

5 In a small bowl, mix together the remaining oil, the vinegar and sugar and season to taste. Pour the dressing over each of the 2 cabbage mixtures and, finally, mix them all together. Serve.

VARIATION

Alternative dressings for this salad can be made with 4 tbsp olive oil, 4 tbsp red wine, 4 tbsp red wine vinegar and 1 tbsp sugar. Or substitute 3 tbsp olive oil and 1 tbsp walnut or hazelnut oil for the olive oil.

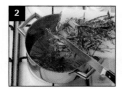

Dolcelatte, Nut & Pasta Salad

Serves 4

INGREDIENTS

225 g/8 oz/2 cups dried pasta
  shells
1 tbsp olive oil
115 g/4 oz/1 cup shelled and
  halved walnuts
mixed salad leaves (greens),
  such as radicchio, escarole,

rocket (arugula), lamb's
  lettuce (corn salad) and
  frisée
225 g/8 oz dolcelatte cheese,
  crumbled
salt

DRESSING:
2 tbsp walnut oil
4 tbsp extra virgin olive oil
2 tbsp red wine vinegar
salt and pepper

1 Bring a large saucepan of lightly salted water to the boil. Add the pasta shells and olive oil and cook until just tender, but still firm to the bite. Drain the pasta, refresh under cold running water, drain thoroughly again and set aside.

2 Spread out the shelled walnut halves on to a baking (cookie) sheet and toast under a preheated grill (broiler) for 2–3 minutes. Set aside to cool.

3 To make the dressing, whisk together the walnut oil, olive oil and vinegar in a small bowl, and season to taste with salt and black pepper.

4 Arrange the salad leaves (greens) in a large serving bowl. Pile the cooled pasta in the middle of the salad leaves (greens) and sprinkle over the dolcelatte cheese. Pour the dressing over the pasta salad, scatter over the walnut halves and toss together to mix. Serve immediately.

COOK'S TIP

Dolcelatte is a semi-soft, blue-veined cheese from Italy. Its texture is creamy and smooth and the flavour is delicate, but piquant. You could substitute Roquefort as an alternative. Whichever cheese you choose, it is essential that it is of the best quality and in peak condition.

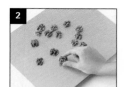

Goat's Cheese with Penne, Pear & Walnut Salad

Serves 4

INGREDIENTS

260 g/9 oz dried penne	2 ripe pears, cored and diced	1 small onion, sliced
5 tbsp olive oil	1 fresh basil sprig	1 large carrot, grated
1 head radicchio, torn into pieces	1 bunch of watercress, trimmed	250 g/9 oz goat's cheese, diced
1 Webbs lettuce, torn into pieces	2 tbsp lemon juice	salt and pepper
7 tbsp chopped walnuts	3 tbsp garlic vinegar	
	4 tomatoes, quartered	

1 Bring a large saucepan of lightly salted water to the boil. Add the penne and 1 tbsp of the olive oil and cook until tender, but still firm to the bite. Drain the pasta, refresh under cold running water, drain thoroughly again and set aside to cool.

2 Place the radicchio and Webbs lettuce in a large salad bowl and mix together well. Top with the pasta, walnuts, pears, basil and watercress.

3 Mix together the lemon juice, the remaining olive oil and the vinegar in a measuring jug (pitcher). Pour the mixture over the salad ingredients and toss to coat the salad leaves well.

4 Add the tomato quarters, onion slices, grated carrot and diced goat's cheese and toss together, using 2 forks, until well mixed. Leave the salad to chill in the refrigerator for about 1 hour before serving.

Pasta & Garlic Mayo Salad

Serves 4

INGREDIENTS

2 large lettuces	juice of 4 lemons	250 ml/9 fl oz/1 1/8 cups fresh
260 g/9 oz dried penne	1 head of celery, sliced	garlic mayonnaise (see
1 tbsp olive oil	115 g/4 oz/3/4 cup shelled,	Cook's Tip, below right)
8 red eating apples	halved walnuts	salt

1 Wash, drain and pat dry the lettuce leaves with kitchen paper (towels). Transfer them to the refrigerator for 1 hour until crisp.

2 Meanwhile, bring a large saucepan of lightly salted water to the boil. Add the pasta and olive oil and cook until tender, but still firm to the bite. Drain the pasta and refresh under cold running water. Drain thoroughly again and set aside.

3 Core and dice the apples, place them in a small bowl and sprinkle with the lemon juice. Mix together the pasta, celery, apples and walnuts and toss the mixture in the garlic mayonnaise (see Cook's Tip, right). Add more mayonnaise, if liked.

4 Line a salad bowl with the lettuce leaves, spoon the pasta salad into the lined bowl and serve.

COOK'S TIP

Sprinkling the apples with lemon juice will prevent them from turning brown.

COOK'S TIP

To make homemade garlic mayonnaise, beat 2 egg yolks with a pinch of salt and 6 crushed garlic cloves. Start beating in 350 ml/ 12 fl oz/1 1/2 cups olive oil, 1–2 tsp at a time, using a balloon whisk or electric mixer. When about one quarter of the oil has been incorporated, beat in 1–2 tbsp white wine vinegar. Continue beating in the oil, adding it in a thin, continuous stream. Finally, stir in 1 tsp Dijon mustard and season to taste.

Fusilli, Avocado, Tomato & Mozzarella Salad

Serves 4

INGREDIENTS

2 tbsp pine nuts (kernels)
175 g/6 oz/1^1/$_2$ cups dried
 fusilli
1 tbsp olive oil
6 tomatoes
225 g/8 oz mozzarella cheese

1 large avocado pear
2 tbsp lemon juice
3 tbsp chopped fresh basil
salt and pepper
fresh basil sprigs, to garnish

DRESSING:
6 tbsp extra virgin olive oil
2 tbsp white wine vinegar
1 tsp wholegrain mustard
pinch of sugar

1 Spread the pine nuts (kernels) out on a baking (cookie) sheet and toast under a preheated grill (broiler) for 1–2 minutes. Remove and set aside to cool.

2 Bring a large saucepan of lightly salted water to the boil. Add the fusilli and olive oil and cook until tender, but still firm to the bite. Drain the pasta and refresh in cold water. Drain again and set aside to cool.

3 Thinly slice the tomatoes and the mozzarella cheese.

4 Cut the avocado pear in half, remove the stone (pit) and skin. Cut into thin slices lengthways and sprinkle with lemon juice to prevent discoloration.

5 To make the dressing, beat together all the dressing ingredients and season to taste with salt and black pepper.

6 Arrange the tomatoes, mozzarella cheese and avocado pear alternately in overlapping slices on a large serving platter.

7 Toss the pasta with half of the dressing and the chopped basil and season to taste. Spoon the pasta into the centre of the platter and pour over the remaining dressing. Sprinkle over the pine nuts (kernels), garnish with fresh basil sprigs and serve.

Pasta-stuffed Tomatoes

Serves 4

INGREDIENTS

5 tbsp extra virgin olive oil,
plus extra for greasing
8 beef tomatoes or large
round tomatoes
115 g/4 oz/1 cup dried ditalini
or other very small pasta
shapes

8 black olives, stoned (pitted)
and finely chopped
2 tbsp finely chopped fresh
basil
1 tbsp finely chopped fresh
parsley

60 g/2 oz/²/₃ cup freshly
grated Parmesan cheese
salt and pepper
fresh basil sprigs, to garnish

1 Brush a baking (cookie) sheet with olive oil.

2 Slice the tops off the tomatoes and reserve to make 'lids'. If the tomatoes will not stand up, cut a thin slice off the bottom of each tomato.

3 Scoop out the tomato pulp into a strainer, but do not pierce the tomato shells. Invert the tomato shells, pat dry and then set aside to drain.

4 Bring a large pan of lightly salted water to the boil. Add the pasta and 1 tbsp of the remaining olive oil and cook until tender, but still firm to the bite. Drain and set aside.

5 Put the olives, chopped basil, parsley and Parmesan cheese into a large mixing bowl and stir in the drained tomato pulp. Add the pasta to the bowl. Stir in the remaining olive oil and season to taste with salt and pepper.

6 Spoon the pasta mixture into the tomato shells and replace the lids. Arrange the tomatoes on the baking (cookie) sheet and bake in a preheated oven at 190°C/375°F/Gas 5 for 15–20 minutes.

7 Remove the tomatoes from the oven and allow to cool until just warm. Arrange on a serving dish, garnish with the fresh basil sprigs and serve.

Rare Beef Pasta Salad

Serves 4

INGREDIENTS

450 g/1 lb rump or sirloin
   steak in one piece
450 g/1 lb dried fusilli
5 tbsp olive oil
2 tbsp lime juice

2 tbsp Thai fish sauce (see
   Cook's Tip, below right)
2 tsp clear honey
4 spring onions (scallions),
   sliced
salt and pepper

1 cucumber, peeled and cut
   into 2.5 cm/1 inch chunks
3 tomatoes, cut into wedges
3 tsp finely chopped fresh
   mint

1 Season the steak with salt and black pepper. Grill (broil) or pan-fry the steak for 4 minutes on each side. Allow to rest for 5 minutes, then slice thinly across the grain.

2 Meanwhile, bring a large saucepan of lightly salted water to the boil. Add the fusilli and 1 tbsp of the olive oil and cook until tender, but still firm to the bite. Drain the fusilli, refresh in cold water and drain again. Toss the fusilli in the remaining oil.

3 Combine the lime juice, fish sauce and honey in a small saucepan and cook over a medium heat for 2 minutes.

4 Add the spring onions (scallions), cucumber, tomatoes and mint to the pan, then add the steak and mix well. Season to taste with salt.

5 Transfer the fusilli to a large, warm serving dish and top with the steak and salad mixture. Serve just warm or allow to cool.

COOK'S TIP

Thai fish sauce, also known as nam pla, *is made from salted anchovies and has quite a strong flavour, so it should be used with discretion. It is available from some supermarkets and from Oriental food stores.*

Beetroot (Beet) Cannolicchi

Serves 4

INGREDIENTS

300 g/11 oz dried ditalini rigati
5 tbsp olive oil
2 garlic cloves, chopped
400 g/14 oz can chopped
   tomatoes

400 g/14 oz cooked beetroot
   (beet), diced
2 tbsp chopped fresh basil
   leaves
1 tsp mustard seeds
salt and pepper

TO SERVE:
mixed salad leaves (greens),
   tossed in olive oil
4 Italian plum tomatoes, sliced

1 Bring a large pan of salted water to the boil. Add the pasta and 1 tbsp of the oil and cook for about 10 minutes, until tender, but still firm to the bite. Drain and set aside.

2 Heat the remaining oil in a large saucepan and fry the garlic for 3 minutes. Add the chopped tomatoes and cook for 10 minutes.

3 Remove the pan from the heat and carefully add the beetroot (beet), basil, mustard seeds and pasta and season to taste with salt and black pepper.

4 Serve on a bed of mixed salad leaves (greens) tossed in olive oil, and sliced plum tomatoes.

COOK'S TIP

Mustard seeds come from three different plants and may be black, brown or white. Black and brown mustard seeds have a stronger, more pungent flavour than white mustard.

COOK'S TIP

To cook raw beetroot (beet), trim off the leaves about 5 cm/2 inches above the root and ensure that the skin is not broken. Boil in very lightly salted water for 30–40 minutes, until tender. Leave to cool and rub off the skin.

Desserts

If when you think about cooking with pasta, desserts do not usually spring to the forefront of your mind, you will be amazed by the wonderfully self-indulgent sweet treats in this chapter. Who could resist Honey & Walnut Nests, a scrumptious combination of pistachio nuts, honey and crisp angel hair pasta? Raspberry Fusilli is a feast for the eyes as well as the tastebuds, German Noodle Pudding is a rich and satisfying dessert based on a traditional Jewish recipe and Baked Sweet Ravioli is a revelation to anyone with a sweet tooth. The recipes in this chapter will convince you that pasta desserts are much more exciting than a macaroni milk pudding and your family and guests will be delighted with such imaginative ways to end a meal.

Baked Sweet Ravioli

Serves 4

INGREDIENTS

PASTA:
425 g/15 oz/3$\frac{3}{4}$ cups plain (all purpose) flour
140 g/5 oz/10 tbsp butter, plus extra for greasing
140 g/5 oz/$\frac{3}{4}$ cup caster (superfine) sugar
4 eggs

25 g/1 oz yeast
125 ml/4 fl oz warm milk

FILLING:
175 g/6 oz/$\frac{2}{3}$ cup chestnut purée
60 g/2 oz/$\frac{1}{2}$ cup cocoa powder

60 g/2 oz/$\frac{1}{4}$ cup caster (superfine) sugar
60 g/2 oz/$\frac{1}{2}$ cup chopped almonds
60 g/2 oz/1 cup crushed amaretti biscuits (cookies)
175 g/6 oz/$\frac{5}{8}$ cup orange marmalade

1 To make the sweet pasta dough, sift the flour into a mixing bowl, then mix in the butter, sugar and 3 eggs.

2 Mix the yeast and warm milk in a small bowl until well combined, then mix into the dough.

3 Knead the dough for 20 minutes, cover with a clean cloth and set aside in a warm place for 1 hour to rise.

4 Combine the chestnut purée, cocoa powder, sugar, almonds, crushed amaretti biscuits (cookies) and orange marmalade in a separate bowl.

5 Grease a baking (cookie) sheet.

6 Lightly flour the work surface (counter). Roll out the pasta dough into a thin sheet and cut into 5 cm/2 inch rounds with a plain pastry cutter.

7 Put a spoonful of filling on to each round and then fold in half, pressing the edges to seal. Arrange on the prepared baking (cookie) sheet, spacing the ravioli out well.

8 Beat the remaining egg and brush all over the ravioli to glaze. Bake in a preheated oven at 180°C/350°F/Gas 4 for 20 minutes until golden. Serve hot.

German Noodle Pudding

Serves 4

INGREDIENTS

60 g/2 oz/4 tbsp butter, plus
   extra for greasing
175 g/6 oz ribbon egg noodles
115 g/4 oz/¹/₂ cup cream
   cheese
225 g/8 oz/1 cup cottage
   cheese

90 g/3 oz/¹/₂ cup caster
   (superfine) sugar
2 eggs, lightly beaten
125 ml/4 fl oz/¹/₂ cup soured
   cream
1 tsp vanilla essence (extract)
a pinch of ground cinnamon

1 tsp grated lemon rind
25 g/1 oz/¹/₄ cup flaked
   (slivered) almonds
25 g/1 oz/³/₈ cup dry
   white breadcrumbs
icing (confectioners') sugar,
   for dusting

1 Grease an ovenproof dish with butter.

2 Bring a large pan of water to the boil. Add the noodles and cook until almost tender. Drain and set aside.

3 Beat together the cream cheese, cottage cheese and caster (superfine) sugar in a mixing bowl. Beat in the eggs, a little at a time, until well combined. Stir in the soured cream, vanilla essence (extract), cinnamon and lemon rind, and fold in the noodles to coat. Transfer the mixture to the prepared dish and smooth the surface.

4 Melt the butter in a frying pan (skillet). Add the almonds and fry, stirring constantly, for about 1–1½ minutes, until lightly coloured. Remove the frying pan (skillet) from the heat and stir the breadcrumbs into the almonds.

5 Sprinkle the almond and breadcrumb mixture over the pudding and bake in a preheated oven at 180°C/350°F/Gas 4 for 35–40 minutes, until just set. Dust with a little icing (confectioners') sugar and serve immediately.

VARIATION

Although not authentic, you could add 3 tbsp raisins with the lemon rind in step 3, if liked.

Honey & Walnut Nests

Serves 4

INGREDIENTS

225 g/8 oz angel hair pasta
115 g/4 oz/8 tbsp butter
175 g/6 oz/1$^{1}/_2$ cups shelled
   pistachio nuts, chopped

115 g/4 oz/$^{1}/_2$ cup sugar
115 g/4 oz/$^{1}/_3$ cup clear honey
150 ml/$^{1}/_4$ pint/$^{5}/_8$ cup water
2 tsp lemon juice

salt
Greek-style yogurt, to serve

1 Bring a large saucepan of salted water to the boil. Add the angel hair pasta and cook until tender, but still firm to the bite. Drain the pasta and return to the pan. Add the butter and toss to coat. Set aside to cool.

2 Arrange 4 small flan or poaching rings on a baking (cookie) sheet. Divide the angel hair pasta into 8 equal quantities and spoon 4 of them into the rings. Press down lightly. Top the pasta with half of the nuts, then add the remaining pasta.

3 Bake in a preheated oven at 180°C/350°F/ Gas 4 for 45 minutes, until golden brown.

4 Meanwhile, put the sugar, honey and water in a saucepan and bring to the boil over a low heat, stirring constantly until the sugar has dissolved completely. Simmer for 10 minutes, add the lemon juice and simmer for a further 5 minutes.

5 Using a palette knife (spatula), carefully transfer the angel hair nests to a serving dish. Pour over the honey syrup, sprinkle over the remaining nuts and set aside to cool completely before serving. Serve with the Greek-style yogurt.

COOK'S TIP

Angel hair pasta is also known as capelli d'Angelo. Long and very fine, it is usually sold in small bunches that already resemble nests.

Raspberry Fusilli

Serves 4

INGREDIENTS

175 g/6 oz/¹/₂ cup fusilli	2 tbsp caster (superfine) sugar	3 tbsp raspberry liqueur
700g/1 lb 9 oz/4 cups	1 tbsp lemon juice	salt
raspberries	4 tbsp flaked almonds	

1 Bring a large pan of lightly salted water to the boil. Add the fusilli and cook until tender, but still firm to the bite. Drain the pasta and return to the pan. Set aside to cool.

2 Using a spoon, firmly press 225 g/ 8 oz/1¹/₃ cups of the raspberries through a sieve (strainer) set over a large mixing bowl to form a smooth purée.

3 Put the raspberry purée and sugar in a small saucepan and simmer over a low heat, stirring occasionally, for 5 minutes.

Stir in the lemon juice then set the sauce aside.

4 Add the remaining raspberries to the fusilli in the pan and mix together well. Transfer the raspberry and fusilli mixture to a serving dish.

5 Spread the almonds out on a baking (cookie) sheet and toast under the grill (broiler) until golden brown. Remove and set aside to cool slightly.

6 Stir the raspberry liqueur into the reserved raspberry sauce

and mix together well until very smooth. Pour the raspberry sauce over the fusilli, sprinkle over the toasted almonds and serve.

VARIATION

You could use almost any sweet, really ripe berry for making this dessert. Strawberries and blackberries are especially suitable, combined with the correspondingly flavoured liqueur. Alternatively, you could use a different berry mixed with the fusilli, but still pour over raspberry sauce.

Index

Index compiled by Hilary Bird.